Rubric Assessment Goes to College

Objective, Comprehensive Evaluation of Student Work

Mary J. Goggins Selke

ROWMAN & LITTLEFIELD EDUCATION

A division of
ROWMAN & LITTLEFIELD PUBLISHERS, INC.
Lanham • New York • Toronto • Plymouth, UK

Published by Rowman & Littlefield Education
A division of Rowman & Littlefield Publishers, Inc.
A wholly owned subsidiary of The Rowman & Littlefield Publishing Group, Inc.
4501 Forbes Boulevard, Suite 200, Lanham, Maryland 20706
www.rowman.com

10 Thornbury Road, Plymouth PL6 7PP, United Kingdom

British Library Cataloguing in Publication Information Available

Library of Congress Cataloging-in-Publication Data
Selke, Mary J. Goggins
 Rubric assessment goes to college : objective, comprehensive evaluation of student work / Mary J. Goggins Selke.
  pages cm
 Includes bibliographical references and index.
 ISBN 978-1-4758-0323-5 (cloth : alk. paper) —ISBN 978-1-4758-0324-2 (pbk. : alk. paper)—ISBN 978-1-4758-0325-9 (electronic) 1. Grading and marking (Students) 2. Education, Higher. I. Title.
 LB2368.S45 2013
 371.27'2—dc23   2012041355

∞^{TM} The paper used in this publication meets the minimum requirements of American National Standard for Information Sciences—Permanence of Paper for Printed Library Materials, ANSI/NISO Z39.48-1992.

Printed in the United States of America

This book is dedicated to Mrs. Florence Healy,
my eight grade English teacher, with love and gratitude
for teaching me the power of "words, words, words."

Contents

Section I: The ABCs of Rubric Assessment

Section II: Designing Rubric Assessments

List of Tables

Preface

Rubric Assessment Goes to College

The first major assignment due for the class that was meeting in room 204 was a position paper worth 20 points, as was clearly stated on the syllabus. After rounds of hesitant questions at the end of every class period, confused e-mail messages, and increasing phone calls to the professor's office as the due date approached, class members submitted their papers. A quick glance through them revealed mediocre work with little evidence of original thought, key components missing, and inconsistent means of organization or citation of sources in text and in the reference list—if sources and a reference list were included.

Most of an entire weekend was spent scoring the papers. Doing so involved repeatedly making the same extensive corrections. Resulting scores ranged from 2 to 17 out of 20 points, with most papers coming in with scores of 12 to 14 points. When the papers were returned the students were clearly disappointed in their scores.

After class there was a long line of students requesting an appointment during the professor's next office hours to discuss the grade they had received. Two students subsequently filed grade appeals; those who had received single-digit scores below 5 points dropped the course. Upon leaving the classroom, the professor overheard a group of students expressing concern that the next assignment was due soon and they still had no idea of what this professor wanted or expected.

The first major assignment due for the class that was meeting in room 206 was also a position paper worth 20 points, as was clearly stated on the syllabus. At the end of every class period the professor asked how the papers were coming along and fielded one or two clarifying questions in person or via e-mail as the due date approached. When class members submitted their papers, they were well organized and professional in appearance. There were frequent attempts at original lines of thought. Key components were addressed. Elements of style were followed when citing sources in text and in the reference list that concluded each paper.

An evening of scoring the papers resulted in a range of scores from 15 to 20 points. The professor had a short list of common errors that were e-mailed to class members as suggestions for fine-tuning future written work. Specific comments on each paper were intended to affirm particular aspects, respond to original ideas, and improve areas of individual challenge. When the papers were returned, students read their feedback and some compared it with the list of common errors they had received by e-mail.

Several students remained after class to dialogue about comments on their papers. Two students who had received 15 points asked if they could make revisions and resubmit their papers. After seeing their rubric scores, they now had a better idea of what the professor wanted and expected.

The differences in what the two groups of professors and students had experienced in the preparation and evaluation of the position papers could be primarily attributed to one key difference: the second syllabus also included the assessment rubric that would be used to score the papers. The rubric included specific, consistent, point-aligned criteria on which the paper would be evaluated. These included clarity and originality of the position taken, key components that needed to be addressed, organization of the paper, and the style sheet to be followed. The style sheet determined the system of citing and documenting the required number and type of references.

Using the rubric helped the students get beyond mechanics to concentrate on the content of the paper. It also saved the professor from the tedium of repeatedly making many of the same corrections, writing long explanations of what had been thought to be readily apparent, or getting so bogged down in addressing mechanical errors that conceptualizations were sidelined. Less time was needed to score the papers and more of that time was devoted to writing feedback pertinent to content, providing encouragement and critical assessment of reasoning, and suggesting additional sources, authors, or approaches to the topic.

The second professor, like the author, has been using rubrics for many years and has never had a grade appealed. Well, that's not quite accurate. I've had a course grade appealed twice in a higher education teaching career that spans more than twenty years. The first appeal happened when a student attended three of the sixteen weekly class sessions in a semester and missed the midterm and final assessment experiences. This was topped off by not responding to my e-mails and phone calls and submitting half of the required projects by slipping them under my office door the day before grades were due. The student in this scenario could not understand why she had been "given" an F in the course.

The second grade appeal involved a department-wide set of rubrics that had been developed before I became a faculty member in the department. The rubrics were not consistently used to hold all students accountable to the expectations set out in the rubrics. As a result, it generated surprise, if not consternation, when my students' grades were based upon the performance levels described in the rubrics. In one instance this resulted in a grade appeal.

Two grade appeals in more than twenty years of working with more than two thousand baccalaureate, master's, post-master's, and doctoral students? Yes. I attribute this to beliefs about assessment that are commensurate with the careful, consistent use of rubrics for assessing major projects and process-based performances in clinical or internship experiences.

Like many of my colleagues in higher education, I am more interested in assessing student learning by authentically evaluating applied knowledge and acquisition of performance skills than in merely assigning grades. Specific feedback on performance measured against a clear set of performance expectations leads to better applied learning for students and better articulation of teaching goals and purposes for faculty members.

HISTORICAL PERSPECTIVE AND THE GENESIS OF MODERN-DAY RUBRICS

My students over the years have known that I tend to provide a good deal of written feedback. However, I rarely use red ink or red electronic font because many students associate red ink with negative grading experiences. This is somewhat ironic, given my experience-based affinity for rubrics, because rubrics have their historical roots in red ink.

The Merriam-Webster Online Dictionary (2012) provides several definitions of the term *rubric*. It is defined as an introductory explanation and as a tradition or custom pertaining to established authoritative rules, especially rules for conducting religious services. It is also explained as the heading of a statute or a heading used to organize the contents of a book or manuscript. The last and apparently most recent definition is that a rubric is "a guide listing specific criteria for grading or scoring academic papers, projects, or tests." The latter definition will serve as a sound starting point for our purposes here.

Historical background pertaining to the genesis of rubrics, in addition to the Merriam-Webster information, may be found on the website of the Frost School of Music at the University of Miami (Asmus, 1999). The English root of the word *rubric* is in the fourteenth-century Middle English *rubrike*, meaning red ocher. This in turn was derived from the thirteenth-century Latin *ruber*, meaning red, or *rubrica*, which means red color or red earth, later translated as *rubrique* in Anglo-French, meaning red chalk.

The actual use of the term *rubric* as a noun was first applied to color-enhanced lines in medieval manuscripts, usually church related, wherein initial letters, whole words, or entire sections of text were printed in red ink for emphasis. Red letters were used in handwritten religious manuscripts, much as highlighting or electronic change tracking are used in contemporary manuscripts, to spotlight important sections or significant names, a practice called *rubrication*. Liturgical directions for priests or ministers were rubricated in service-related prayer books, similar to the way stage instructions are often italicized in the script of a play.

Red typeface is still used in many religious service books today to differentiate between words to be spoken by celebrants and words to be spoken by members of the congregation during prayers or ceremonies. In historical legal documents, text in red type was also used in some cases to highlight headings in code law. This connection to written directions in religious texts or to formal requirements of the law forms the basis for the current use of the term *rubric* as a set of specific directions for observation-based assessment.

I first learned the basics of rubric assessment from members of the English Department at Fort Dodge Senior High School in Fort Dodge, Iowa, while serving as university supervisor for a University of Northern Iowa student teacher at the school in spring 1993. The genesis of assessment rubrics for PK–12 usage actually dates back almost two decades prior to that time.

Rubrics were used to assess developmental aspects of children's drawings for the New York State Education Department in 1978. This was soon followed, in 1979, by the use of assessment rubrics for the New York State Regents' natural language writing competency test. The systems of rubric assessment made the inherently subjective more objective and facilitated more consistent evaluation of student work. Rubrics caught on, initially among American educators and then among education professionals and associations around the world.

Assessment rubrics were originally used primarily by teachers in kindergarten through high school. Universities, state departments of education, and commercial providers continue to maintain websites that feature rubrics of varying quality for assessing PK–12 student work in curricular content areas and in cocurricular areas as well such as character development, leadership, and service-learning. Several books also exist to provide tips and examples for developing and using rubrics, mostly at the PK–12 levels (Arter, 2006; Arter & McTighe, 2001; Burke, 2011; Quinlan, 2006; Stevens & Levi, 2005).

In the past decade, higher education accrediting bodies and college or university departments, outside as well as inside academic units, have begun using rubrics for the evaluation of programs and students within them. A recent example would be the Association of American Colleges and Universities' Valid Assessment of Learning in Undergraduate Education (VALUE) project. Assessment rubrics were developed for the association's fifteen liberal learning outcomes, published in their *Assessing Outcomes and Improving Achievement: Tips and Tools for Using Rubrics* (2010). Rubric assessment instruments for program and unit review are also used by professional associations and accrediting organizations such as the Accrediting Commission for Community and Junior Colleges (2011) and the National Council for the Accreditation of Teacher Education (2008).

On campuses across the United States and beyond, departments or schools of business, education, liberal arts, management, medical professions, pharmacy, and physical or social sciences are beginning to use rubrics to assess student progress and the effective implementation of programmatic components. This book is intended as a guide to assist instructors and administrators in the development of high-quality assessment rubrics.

REFERENCES

Accrediting Commission for Community and Junior Colleges (2011). Rubric for evaluating institutional effectiveness. Retrieved from http://www.accjc.org/wp-content/uploads/2011/10/CoverMemoAndRevisedRubric_10-28-2011.pdf.

Arter, J. A. (2006). *Creating and recognizing quality rubrics*. Boston: Allyn & Bacon.

Arter, J. A., & McTighe, J. (2001). *Scoring rubrics in the classroom: Using performance criteria for assessing and improving student performance*. Thousand Oaks, CA: Corwin.

Asmus, E. (1999). Rubrics: Definition, benefits, history, and types. Retrieved from http://www.music.miami.edu/assessment/rubricsDef.html.

Association of American Colleges and Universities (2010). *Assessing outcomes and improving achievement: Tips and tools for using rubrics*. Washington, DC.

Burke, K. (2011). *From standards to rubrics in six steps: Tools for assessing student learning* (3rd ed.). Thousand Oaks, CA: Corwin.

Merriam-Webster Online Dictionary (2012). Rubric. Retrieved from http://www.merriam-webster.com/dictionary/rubric.

National Council for the Accreditation of Teacher Education (2008). NCATE unit standards Retrieved from http://www.ncate.org/Standards/NCATEUnitStandards/UnitStandardsinEffect2008/tabid/476/Default.aspx.

Quinlan, A. (2006). *A complete guide to rubrics: Assessment made easy for teachers, K–college*. Lanham, MD: Rowman & Littlefield.

Stevens, D. D., & Levi, A. J. (2005). *Introduction to rubrics: An assessment tool to save grading time, convey effective feedback, and promote student learning*. Sterling, VA: Stylus.

Acknowledgments

"At times our own light goes out and is rekindled by a spark from another person. Each of us has cause to think with deep gratitude of those who have lighted the flame within us."

—Albert Schweitzer

I would be remiss if I didn't thank several writers and personal "spark re-kindlers" who have been wonderfully supportive during the production phase of this book. You all know why you are mentioned here, in no particular order except alphabetical. To Peggy Ishler Bosse, Mark Grauer, Wanda Ramm, Jim Selke, Meghan Selke, Leigh Zeitz, and my beloved personal muse—my respect and deepest appreciation.

And finally my thanks to Tom Koerner at Rowman & Littlefield and Patti Belcher, formerly of Rowman & Littlefield, for not giving up on this author. And for not letting me give up on this project.

Introduction

How This Book Is Organized

With the burgeoning interest in rubric assessment for multiple purposes at the postsecondary level, this book has been developed as a practical, comprehensive resource for rubric design, analysis, and application at the postsecondary level. Multiple examples of rubrics and of rubrics in construction are provided throughout the book. At the end of each chapter, the conceptual highlights are captured in a section on key considerations.

SECTION ONE: THE ABCS OF RUBRIC ASSESSMENT

In the first section in the book, the case is made for rubric assessment in chapter 1 (Advantages of Rubrics: What They Can Do for You). In chapter 2 (Basis for Assessment: Performance or Product) the advantages of rubrics for assessing performances or products are presented. In chapter 3 (Categories of Rubrics: Analytic and Holistic) the two primary categories of rubrics, analytic and holistic, are addressed through foundational explanations and examples of postsecondary teaching and evaluation tasks that lend well to rubric assessment.

SECTION TWO: DESIGNING RUBRIC ASSESSMENTS

In the second section in the book, construction elements are emphasized. This begins with chapter 4 (Matching Tool to Task, or When a Rubric Is Not the Best Option) on matching assessment tools to assessment tasks, including alternatives to rubric assessment when a rubric is not the best fit. It is followed by chapter 5 (Rubric Design: Analytic Rubrics), in which the basics of rubric design are presented in ten specific steps for creating analytic rubrics. In chapter 6 (Rubric Design: Holistic Rubrics) the ten steps in rubric construction are tailored to holistic rubrics. In chapter 7 (A Closer Look at Rubric Strand Design) readers will be able to delve deeper into strand development, a pivotal element of rubric construction. In chapter 8 (Common Errors in Rubric Design) the underlying reasons for problems in rubric construction and implementation are explored. When higher education faculty members are reluctant to use rubrics, prior experience with a rubric plagued by one of these errors is often the reason. Eliminating these concerns strengthens the effectiveness of rubrics, and awareness of them provides for an informed choice if a rubric is designed with one or more of the common errors in play.

SECTION THREE: IMPLEMENTING RUBRIC ASSESSMENTS

The third section of the book begins with chapter 9 (Converting Rubric Scores to Grades), in which guidance is provided for converting rubric scores to percentages or letter grades for individual assignments or for entire courses. Chapter 10 (Designing a Standards-Aligned Rubric) features options for developing rubrics that incorporate state or national standards into rubric assessment instruments. In chapter 11 (Additional Rubric Uses), the final chapter in the book, the focus is moved off the assessment of student work. The ten steps of rubric construction are applied to the design of a rubric meant to bring increased clarity and subjectivity to the process of screening job applicants. The book is concluded with a brief annotated bibliography.

The resulting book is an asset for university, professional school, college, community college, and upper-level secondary school faculty members wishing to gain a practical, comprehensive working knowledge of rubric design, analysis, and implementation. It can be used for faculty professional development or as a resource for personnel who work with new, returning, or relocating faculty members.

It will also be effective as a supplemental textbook in courses on assessment in postsecondary settings or as a personal guide to rubric usage at the college or university level. In short, this book provides one-stop rubric shopping for specifics in rubric design. Essential concepts, common issues and problems, design, implementation, standards alignment, and grade-focused applications of rubric assessment in higher education contexts will be addressed through specific examples and tools for rubric design and implementation.

1

THE ABCs OF RUBRIC ASSESSMENT

1

Advantages of Rubrics

What They Can Do for You

Assessment is a term used by everyone who teaches at the college or university level. But if you were to ask a dozen of your colleagues to define the term, you would most likely be the recipient of a dozen widely varied definitions. Try it—the question may facilitate some lively debate, and you'll quickly see what I mean. To some, assessment is synonymous with "giving" grades. To others, it refers to the formative process that occurs before a final evaluation or perhaps the summative process that takes place to determine final percentage scores or letter grades.

There may be colleagues who think of assessment only in the very formal context of a standardized paper-and-pencil or electronically administered test. Other colleagues may think of it as the ongoing informal checking in they do with students to see how their students are doing on a major paper or project. Still others think of assessment as an accounting of how much factual information has been absorbed by their students.

Teaching at times does involve determining how much theoretical information has been committed to memory. However, if our roles as college, university, or professional school instructors were to be limited to that function of assessment, we could all quickly and easily be replaced by testing devices that do not require health or life insurance policies. Grading measures—be they letter grades, traditional percentage scores based on a high score of 100, course point totals, or competency designations—are important components of the assessment process, but they should not be considered synonymous with it in terms of the instructor-student dynamic.

To an extent that varies by content area, topic, class, and course of study, being college, university, or professional school instructors also requires teaching students how to critically analyze, apply, and build on information.

This is essential if students are to acquire a working knowledge of the concepts and skills in our respective disciplines.

The kinds of teaching that lay a foundation for the ongoing acquisition of skills and knowledge need assessment methods that support process as well as product and involve formative as well as summative assessment. Instructors that buy into this kind of teaching need assessment methods that facilitate breaking complex tasks into more readily identifiable components and tracking progress as well as rewarding mastery. Assessment methods are also needed that show students what they are doing right, what they are doing wrong, and what they specifically must do to improve.

Assessment and evaluation instruments that address more than the acquisition of knowledge are essential if we are to go beyond the traditional academic role of dispensing theoretical knowledge. Assessment tools are needed to carry the profession forward into the realm of ensuring that students know what to do with knowledge and how to apply it in practice.

COMMUNICATION TOOL

That is where rubrics come in because they are a tool that can help accomplish many of the tasks inherent in the assessment of working knowledge. In essence, an assessment process is a communication process that takes place between instructors and students. Instructors provide performance expectations in course syllabi. Students use the syllabi and accompanying explanations as a basis for determining what they will need to do in order to accomplish the performance tasks that are expected as course requirements. The more clearly expectations are communicated, the better chance students have of meeting them.

NO-SURPRISES ASSESSMENT

Success in providing clear expectations would probably be found to have a direct inverse correlation with the anxiety levels experienced by students after they leave classrooms or online course rooms for the first time and attempt to figure out what will be required of them. Readers may know or have known colleagues who actually enjoy keeping their students guessing. A rubric won't be a good fit in those situations because a rubric facilitates no-surprises assessment.

Rubrics for major projects, performance tasks, or papers are ideally provided along with the syllabus. If that is not possible, rubrics are provided well in advance of when students would need to begin working on whatever the rubrics will be used to assess.

CLEAR EXPECTATIONS

The instructor may design and provide a rubric. Students may be asked to assist with its development. Academic colleagues may collaborate on the design of a rubric to be used in one or more multiple-section courses. The rubric may be borrowed or adapted from a print or online source. Regardless of who designs it, students and instructor alike need to have a copy of the rubric before beginning the performance task to be assessed.

Everyone involved needs to know precisely what the expectations are for the task(s) at hand. The author once had a colleague who was frankly appalled at this idea. Upon introduction to rubrics in a faculty development presentation, the professor said, "This is preposterous! What would happen if *all* of our students achieved at our highest level of expectations?" The response to this remains the same as if a more indirect approach (and what was hoped at the time would be a less tenure-suicidal approach) had not been taken: "And the problem with that would be . . . ?"

CONSISTENCY AND FAIRNESS

In addition to making expectations clear from the beginning, rubric assessment can assist in ensuring that instructor expectations are consistent, fair, and equitable from one student to another. Student concerns regarding perceived favoritism or inconsistent interpretation of what will be required over the course of a class can be greatly alleviated if not dispelled by using well-designed rubric assessment instruments. The same set of assessment requirements applies to everyone. If the rubric is altered in any way for one student, it is altered for other students in the same manner.

EQUITABLE OPTIONS

That being said, it is possible to provide more than one means of demonstrating competence that could be assessed on the same rubric. Equitable does not mean inflexible. At first glance, this might be perceived as different rules for different students, but in actuality it is a means of differentiating instruction for individual students in a class.

In one case, graduate students were provided the option of writing a program capstone paper describing their original research or going through the process of submitting an article on their research to a refereed journal for possible publication. Only one student opted for the journal article route, initially attracted by the shorter length of the document that would need to be prepared. The student subsequently discovered that this option was actually more work intensive—a concern that quickly diminished when the article was accepted for publication.

In another case, an undergraduate student could not participate in a required field component of a course due to work commitments beyond the student's control on the day in question. An alternate arrangement was proposed and agreed to by the instructor that would permit the student to demonstrate the same set of skills.

OBJECTIVE CRITERIA

In addition to making assessment processes consistent and equitable from student to student, rubric assessment provides an opportunity to make what can be inherently subjective more objective. The use of rubrics in PK–12 settings originated in the field of English/language arts for good reason. Many of the assessment tasks falling to English instructors at all levels, kindergarten to college, involve the evaluation and coaching of written documents.

Assessing a document composed of written narrative, be it a research paper, essay exam, observation notes, or a science lab write-up, involves more complex processes than scoring a true-false, multiple choice, or short answer test. Instructors may also face the inherent challenge of remaining objective despite the students' choices of specific topics, viewpoints, or lines of reasoning. It can be a challenge to separate the topic from the writing process in order to critique an argument objectively. This may be compounded if a student is writing in support of something an instructor opposes or that goes against a deeply held belief. Rubrics can be of assistance in focusing more objectively on the required knowledge and skills demonstrated through components of the written work regardless of the topic.

OBSERVABLE REQUIREMENTS

The emphasis on objective, observable performance components is also helpful when meeting with students who question a grade received on an assignment for which there was a scoring rubric. The conversation can be steered away from variations on the theme of, "Why did you give me such a low grade?" to helping students see why their *work* was scored the way it was on the rubric. This changes the focus from the individual or any subjective perceptions of personal differences to a more objective focus on specified requirements for the work to be accomplished.

DISTINCT STRENGTHS AND WEAKNESSES

The elements inherent in rubric design can also be helpful when students perform very well in some areas and are challenged in others. For example, it is possible for students to be very facile with the mechanics of punctuation, grammar, spelling, and subject-verb agreement yet have difficulty stating a position on a topic and supporting it. The reverse can also be true. It is also possible for students to submit five-page essays that are very well written—except that they consist of one five-page paragraph, beginning to end.

In the old days of assessment, these circumstances could easily have resulted in a frustrating sequence of C papers for the student. Content would have rated an A while mechanics would have rated an F. Unless it was the practice of the instructor to provide two scores, one for mechanics and one for content, the unfortunate student would have seen an abundance of red ink on the paper. As a result, the student would probably think he or she was doing everything wrong rather than some things very well and others not. More important, the student may not have known where to begin in order to improve.

When a rubric is used, students can see how they performed on specific components of the overall assessment task. They can also see what specific components would need to be improved, and what this would look like, in order to perform at a higher, more accomplished level.

RELATIVE IMPORTANCE OF TASK COMPONENTS

Breaking the overall assessment task into specific components does help students to better understand what the task will involve. It also helps students to see what they will need to do in order to accomplish a task at an acceptable level of performance and to identify the key components of the overall task. If a component is important enough to have a strand devoted to it on the rubric, it is clear that this component must be competently addressed when completing the overall performance task.

Likewise, if a given component is not mentioned, or is addressed along with other components rather than standing alone, it sends the message that this component is not as essential to the overall assessment task at hand. For example, specific style requirements in terms of cover page and abstract may make up a rubric strand for an undergraduate paper, but in graduate-level papers these would be a given and would not be specifically addressed via a rubric strand.

As another example, in an introductory course encompassing graduate-level writing expectations, specific components of APA (or MLA, etc.) style may each be considered on individual rubric strands. However, assignments in subsequent graduate courses may address APA considerations through one rubric strand for APA mechanics and another for using appropriate APA citations in text and in the reference list. The specificity of rubrics help students understand what it will take to accomplish an assessment task, what is important, and what is not.

DISPOSITIONAL BEHAVIORS

In many cases, however, some of what is important in an assessment task is intangible and cannot be directly observed. Quite often in these cases, whether or not a student achieves an acceptable performance level cannot be explicated clearly enough to stand up in a grade appeal or, for that matter, in court.

Some of the most fundamental aspects of many disciplines are dispositional. How does one accurately measure a social work student's sense of personal integrity or professional ethics? A medical student's ability to get patients to trust him or her enough to fully disclose symptoms or prior diagnoses when discussing their medical histories? An education major's commitment to providing the best possible education for all students, not just for those who come from backgrounds similar to his or her own? The dispositions may not be tangible or observable, but the kinds of behaviors that result from these intangible components can often be observed.

For example, business students majoring in marketing may be given a written or electronic test to assess their theoretical knowledge of business ethics. Assessing their working knowledge of ethics would involve an assessment of their observed conduct in business transactions rather than a decontextualized test on ethics.

Marketing students at Lakeland College in Wisconsin are required to consistently demonstrate their ability to clearly articulate such things as product/service full disclosures and the potential and limitations of a given product or service to potential consumers and colleagues. This needs to be done within a context of what a consumer's real needs may or may not be, what the product or service can and cannot do for a potential buyer, and whether or not the product or service will likely meet a specific potential buyer's real needs (J. Kudek, personal communication, January 10, 2011). In this case, the demonstrable behaviors associated with ethical dispositions could be addressed on a performance assessment instrument.

FORMATIVE OR SUMMATIVE ASSESSMENT

Another strength of rubrics is that they can be used for formative, work-in-progress assessment or for final, summative assessment purposes. Although they can work perfectly well as summative, final assessments, rubrics are formative by nature. Their emphasis is on specifying a developmental range of observable performance behaviors.

For example, in assessing clinical experiences, higher rubric scores commensurate with more advanced demonstration of skills on the same rubric strand components may be required to remain in good standing toward the end of a clinical rotation or semester than what may have been required in the initial weeks. In another example of using a rubric to assess developing skills, the same rubric may be used to assess a series of four papers written for a freshman composition class. Increasingly higher rubric scores are required for translation into grades of A, B, and C on those papers as the semester progresses and students hopefully become more skilled in demonstrating the rubric strand components assessed.

Despite the inherently formative nature of rubrics, they also lend well to summative assessment, clarifying what must be demonstrated to earn specific scores for the final overall course grade. Sometimes the same rubric may be used for formative and summative assessment purposes within the same course or program.

Building on the above example of assessing clinical experiences, the same rubric that will be used to determine the final clinical-assessment grade could be introduced at the beginning of the clinical experience. Students would have a clear picture of where they are heading and what levels of skill will need to be demonstrated by the end of the practicum. The same rubric assessment instrument can be used as a basis for formal or informal evaluation conferences throughout the experience. When this kind of consistency is provided, student and instructor usually know what the final grade for the clinical experience will be—and why—by the time the final grade needs to be formally computed and reported.

VARIED ENTRY-LEVEL SKILLS

In classes where students come in with widely varied backgrounds or skill levels, an assessment rubric can permit the instructor to more accurately pinpoint the progress made by each student. Rubrics also facilitate taking students where they are upon entering the course and helping them move forward from there. This can be a challenge, especially in large classes, but it can be done.

When the author was a doctoral student, back in the pre-rubric era, enrolling in the first (required) philosophy course ever taken resulted in joining a class wherein some of the other students had majored or minored in philosophy as undergraduates. Although I came in as a novice, the course content was fascinating. It also necessitated sitting up front so as not to miss anything, to enjoy the professor's animated lecture style, and to decrease chances of napping during the long, warm afternoons of the compacted course.

One memorable afternoon toward the end of the first of four weeks, the class saw the professor expound on the Allegory of the Cave. Before realizing the words had been spoken aloud, the author said, "That is *so* cool!"—at which point the instructor closed his notes less than gently and even less gently asked if the author had ever had a philosophy class before. Responding, "No, but I am really enjoying this one!" resulted in the instructor calling for a five-minute break. An impromptu professor-student conference was held in the hallway outside the classroom.

The instructor did not change the performance expectations and should not have been expected to do so. However, he did invest extra effort by providing supplemental readings and frequent "how is it going?" communication during breaks to be sure his naively enthusiastic student progressed. He was dedicated to facilitating the progress of every student from an individualized point *a* to point *b*. This was true for his outspoken philosophy enthusiast as well, despite the fact that her entry-level point *a* was lower than that of most students in the class.

A grade of B in the course was earned by the outspoken student. When asked why, the instructor explained that if the grade had been based solely on amount of progress made over the past month it would have been an A. If a rubric had been used to determine the overall course grade, it may still have been a B, given the large amount of conceptual ground to cover in those four weeks. However, the student in question would have known the specific skills that had been acquired. What was needed to reach the level needed for an A would have been explicit, and the final grade probably would not have been questioned. A rubric in this instance could also have served as a guide for self-monitored ongoing study after the course concluded.

Use of a rubric would have been a good fit for this professor's commitment to helping all students learn, no matter their entry levels. The instructor would have been better able to account not only for overall knowledge attained but also for student progress in regard to developmental processes pertinent to specific components of working knowledge embedded in the course. Both aspects would have been helpful for computing and communicating final grades in the course.

COURSE GRADES AS WELL AS PROJECT GRADES

In addition to using them for the evaluation of primary performance tasks in the course, the use of rubrics for determining composite course grades may be the ultimate use of rubrics for summative assessment purposes. Through the lens of a rubric, summative assessment involves recording the rubric-based scores for major assessment tasks in the course, adding points for any additional requirements that were not assessed with a rubric, if applicable, and providing a final point total score that is a composite of the formative scores achieved throughout the course. The final score can then be converted into a numerical percentage or letter grade, using a variety of simple methods. (This is addressed in chapter 9.)

Whether used for formative or summative assessment, rubrics can be extremely helpful to instructors and to their students. This is the case regardless of whether rubrics are used to assess a demonstration of skill or the production of a tangible project. The advantages of rubrics are summarized in the key considerations for this chapter.

However, as a quick recap—are you seeking an assessment tool to help you and your students clarify expectations, focus on the work, identify strengths as well as areas of challenge, and make what can be inherently subjective more objective? If so, welcome to the world of assessment rubrics and to the remaining chapters of this book. As mentioned in the introduction, the book was designed to provide one-stop rubric shopping. Do you want no-nonsense how-tos, rubric examples, and insight into the decision-making processes of rubric design? Furthermore, do you want to develop or expand the working knowledge you need to construct, revise, and implement rubrics? If so—read on! Glad to be of assistance. You have come to the right place to find the right tools for the job of objective, comprehensive assessment.

KEY CONSIDERATIONS: ADVANTAGES OF RUBRICS

- Rubrics function as a communication tool to clarify performance expectations. The more clearly we communicate our expectations, the better chance our students have of meeting them.

- Rubrics are ideally provided along with the syllabus or, if that is not possible, well in advance of when students would need to begin working so that student and professor can plan ahead.
- Rubrics help ensure everyone knows the requirements so that expectations are consistent, fair, and equitable; equitable does not mean inflexible.
- Rubrics provide opportunities to make what can be inherently subjective more objective by focusing on specific requirements for the work to be accomplished.
- Rubrics show students how they performed on specific components of the assessment task, what components need to be improved, and how to do so in order to perform at a more accomplished level.
- Rubrics help students understand what the task will involve, what they will need to do in order to accomplish it, and what the important components of the overall task will involve.
- Rubrics can provide a means to score student dispositions that may not be tangible or observable but that can be observed in the kinds of behaviors that result from these intangible components.
- Rubrics can be used as developmental guides as well as for the primary purposes of providing formative, work-in-progress assessment or final, summative assessment.
- Rubrics can assist the instructor to more accurately pinpoint the progress made by each student, especially in classes where students come in with widely varied backgrounds or skill levels.
- Rubrics may be used to determine composite course grades in addition to using them for the evaluation of primary performance tasks in the course.

2

Basis for Assessment

Performance or Product

Rubrics are used for two kinds of assessment tasks: those that involve performance processes that are enacted and those that involve concrete artifacts that are produced. Examples of performance tasks involving assessment of enacted skills would be rubrics designed to document student progress and achievement in field experiences, internships, clinical rotations, laboratory sections of courses, or service-learning experiences.

The most common examples of a performance task pertinent to product or artifact assessment would include rubrics constructed to document student progress and achievement in producing written essays or research papers. Additional examples of product-focused rubrics would include creating musical compositions, theatrical scripts, or paintings; designing unit lesson plans for elementary, middle, or secondary schools; or writing legal briefs.

Whether one is assessing performance or product, there are three characteristics pertinent to a high-quality, effective rubric. Criteria described in the rubric strands must be (1) essential to the performance or product production task, (2) attainable by the student(s) whose work is being assessed, and (3) reflective of observable proficiency levels specific to each criterion.

PERFORMANCE TASK RUBRICS

Performance task rubrics are designed to aid in the assessment of student work that focuses on demonstration of a specific skill or set of skills rather than on the production of a tangible product. The focus can be formative, concentrating on the assessment of the skills during the development phase, or summative, focusing on the skills when they are expected to be fully developed. Demonstration of the skills results in one or more desired outcomes, but the process outcomes, while they are observable, are not static. They are not able to be placed on a professor's desk or on public display in final, tangible two- or three-dimensional form. Try thinking of performance or process as something that would require a video clip rather than a snapshot to capture its essence.

For example, if a student in a medical or veterinary field is learning the process for inserting and starting an IV line, there are readily observable skills pertinent to this process. The desired outcome is a safe, comfortable, secured, functioning IV. The end result of performing the set of skills necessary to achieve this end is observable. But the process leading up to the final result is not something that can be put into a box or briefcase, carried into a clinical professor's office, and set on the professor's desk so that it can be assessed.

It is performance-based rather than product-based. While a picture could be taken of what happens to a patient's arm, hand, or foreleg when an IV is or is not successfully inserted and started, the student is being assessed on how well he or she enacts the whole process of getting the line in and the IV running. A video clip, rather than a picture, would be needed to show how well the student performed the process that results in the outcome. A performance-based rubric would be needed to assess that process.

PERFORMANCE TASK: ESSENTIAL CRITERIA

A general rule of thumb for performance rubrics is to include only those elements that are essential to the process(es) to be evaluated. Elements that are peripheral do not belong in a performance rubric. For example, a rubric may be constructed to assess the end of semester presentation by theater students in a directing class. A rubric designed to be used when assessing the overall performance task of directing a scene from a play would also address the work done in the weeks leading up to the presentation of the scene.

The final product will certainly be indicative of the directing and coaching processes that have come before. Elements such as working with individual actors to develop their characters and the full cast to develop their characters' relationships with each other, coaching vocal production and diction, blocking the movement and action on the stage, and communicating to the actors what the director needs or wants from them would all be criteria essential to direction.

The decision to specify every movement, breath, or speech inflection or give the actors the freedom to experiment and bring their own ideas and interpretations into the process of developing the scene would comprise additional choices made in the directing process. The two extremes may end up on opposite sides of a rubric's midpoint depending on the theater professor's definition of what constitutes effective direction in general or for a scene of the kind the student director is producing. The important thing is that the theater instructor clearly specifies what essential elements are involved in the developmental process of learning to direct by focusing on them in the design of an assessment rubric.

Following the same example, the actors' costumes and makeup, the set design, the stage lighting, and the amplification or sound effects are all important to overall theatrical production. All are certainly within the scope of the director's influence. There may be other rubrics that address these elements if the theater professor chooses to include them. However, in an assessment instrument focused purely on the performance tasks pertinent to directing actors on the stage, these elements are peripheral to the performance task at hand.

The elements would be outweighed—in number, points assigned to them, or their lack of presence on an assessment instrument—by criteria that are essential and directly pertinent to the process of directing. Aspects of production such as producing the program or advertisement posters, while components relevant to the production of a show, would be completely peripheral in this case. They would not be included on a rubric designed to address essential elements of the directing process.

PERFORMANCE TASK: ATTAINABILITY

Rubrics, or individual rubric strands, that set out performance tasks that are not within the reach of the students whose performances the rubric will be used to evaluate would also not be included. This seems to go without saying, and the reader may wonder why it is mentioned at all. Instructors often provide experiences that are intended to stretch their students, take them beyond their comfort zones, give them a sample of an experience that is not yet within their capability. Doing so is a time-honored part of the educational process. However, using a rubric or any other evaluation instrument to assess competence levels in an area where a student cannot yet be expected to demonstrate competence, or at a level that cannot yet be reasonably expected of the student, is an anxiety-producing exercise in frustration for the student and ultimately for the instructor as well.

For example, a college freshman once received a tour of the research library on a major university campus when visiting a respected former teacher. The student's teacher had become a graduate student at the university and was working toward a doctorate in music. They got out of the elevator on the floor that housed hard copies of doctoral dissertations. The teacher responded to the student's questions about what they were and why they were written, then pulled a few from the shelves as examples.

The student looked through them and read a few paragraphs, noting similarities in the ways the same numbered chapters were organized from one dissertation to another. The similarities were compared to the formulaic rules used for writing fugues in music. When the student mentioned it would be cool to write a dissertation someday, the teacher smiled and replied, "You could—you probably will." The bound copies of the dissertations were put back on the shelves. It was a taste, an intriguing introduction, and one that never left the student, who did earn a doctoral degree years later.

However, if a rubric or any other evaluation instrument had been used to assess the student's knowledge of the elements that made up the chapters of a traditional dissertation at that point, it would have been premature. One of the student's doctoral research professors would do this sixteen years later, but it would have been out of line with what could be expected of a second-semester college freshman.

An entering undergraduate does not possess the background, the working knowledge, or the bank of experiences necessary to perform that kind of analysis. Not yet. However, if a doctoral research professor would choose to use a rubric to assess a doctoral student's ability to analyze and describe the components in the traditional chapters of a dissertation? It would be an attainable performance task, well within the realm of what could reasonably be expected of a predissertation doctoral student.

PERFORMANCE TASK: DEVELOPMENTAL LEVELS

A key strength of rubric assessment is its utility to specify the observable behaviors inherent in the steps leading from fledgling performance to full competence that meets or exceeds expectations. The primary challenge here is to be sure that a developmental phase is not overlooked in the process of defining the developmental levels.

In actual practice, development occurs more on a continuum than in neatly defined cells on a rubric strand. The trick in converting an ongoing continuum into pinpointed developmental levels lies in the ability to define the specific behaviors to be observed and then to draft language that describes them in the number of cells desired for the rubric. After this process is completed, the rubric may be piloted to test comprehensive usefulness when working with actual demonstrations of these skills. If performance situations arise that do not fit the description of any of the cells in the drafted rubric, the instrument will need to be revised as needed until all performance behaviors pertinent to each rubric strand will fit clearly into one of the cells.

CONCRETE ARTIFACT/PRODUCT RUBRICS

Product-related rubrics are designed to aid in the assessment of student work that focuses on the development and construction of specific, tangible artifacts. These products can also be assessed in progress or when completed, using a formative assessment instrument or a summative assessment instrument, just as is the case for performance-related outcomes. While skills will be needed to create the desired product, the outcome in a product-related demonstration of applied knowledge is static—two- or three-dimensional. It could be placed on a professor's desk, viewed on display in a public setting, or submitted as an electronic file.

For example, imagine a class of art students was contracted to design and produce a large metal sculpture to be displayed on campus. Specified components would need to be included in the sculpture. Their art professor would certainly want to observe and coach the process of constructing the sculpture. Indeed, rubric strands related to process may be part of a formative assessment rubric for this project.

However, the main point of this assignment is to produce that sculpture. The concrete product is the sculpture. The end result of performing the set of skills necessary to achieve this goal is not only observable, it is a stand-alone product that can be displayed on campus. It is product focused rather than performance focused. A picture could be taken of the final product. A video clip is not needed to present the end result. The final product is a concrete, tangible entity.

ARTIFACT/PRODUCT PRODUCTION: ESSENTIAL CRITERIA

As is the case for performance rubrics, a general rule of thumb for artifact/product rubrics is to include only those elements that are essential to the tangible products to be evaluated. Elements that are peripheral do not belong in the rubric. For instance, when assessing student research papers, instructors would want to focus on elements such as specified topics or aspects of the topics, answers to questions, or the components required in specific sections of the paper.

For example, when the author's graduate students propose a research topic, it is required that they present it in "P–Q–P" format. They first need to provide a paragraph outlining the research *problem*: the initial "P." They are then required to state the overriding research *question*: the "Q." The third component needed is the intended *purpose* of the research: the second "P."

Background information not relevant to a concise description of the research problem is peripheral to the focal components and is not needed for purposes of the P–Q–P description, although it may be needed for purposes of a fully developed research project. Components such as definitions of terms, which will also be an important component of a fully developed research project, or for that matter a full proposal, are also not essential at this point and would not be addressed in a performance rubric developed for the purpose of assessing the P–Q–P.

ARTIFACT/PRODUCT PRODUCTION: ATTAINABILITY

Continuing with the same example, class time is devoted to identifying the P–Q–P in research studies the students read in professional refereed journals. This starts in their initial graduate-level courses and continues with formulating P–Q–P summaries for hypothetical research studies. By the time graduate students progress to the point of enrolling in a research course, they are familiar with the terms and have seen myriad examples from quantitative and qualitative sources. They have also had opportunity to critique and edit examples of P–Q–P statements, and have participated in collaborative processes of drafting P–Q–P summaries.

By the time the candidates are asked to formulate their own P–Q–P for purposes of expanding it into a fully developed research proposal, they have had ample opportunities to practice and work with the concepts. This prepares them to be able to produce the desired product: a concise, specific, credible, researchable P–Q–P.

The same rubric that will be used to assess their personal products was provided from the very beginning for purposes of critiquing and eventually editing the quality of P–Q–Ps they had encountered up to that point. However, the rubric was not initially used to evaluate their own products, at least not for a grade that will become part of their course grades. This was not done until they had developed enough skill to have the production of the desired P–Q–P artifact be a reasonably attainable goal.

ARTIFACT/PRODUCT PRODUCTION: DEVELOPMENTAL LEVELS

The process of designing a rubric to address the developmental levels pertinent to product or artifact design may actually be easier than drafting a rubric to address developmental levels of a skill. If anything, it may be much simpler to get a visual image of what a product looks like from the point of being unsatisfactory to that of being exemplary. It is also to be expected that the developmental levels expressed in the rubric will be dependent upon the quality of the product attainable for a given student or group of students.

For example, what constitutes an unsatisfactory, developing, satisfactory, excellent, or exemplary level of performance on a rubric designed to assess a twenty-page research paper would be very different for a college freshman and for a master's or doctoral student. This is the case because a developmentally appropriate outcome would differ for undergraduate students as contrasted with graduate students. This would be the case even if the criteria to be addressed, listed down the far left-hand column of the rubric, were identical.

COMBINING PERFORMANCE AND PRODUCT

Rubrics offer additional potential for applications in higher education or upper secondary settings that combine the two functions and capitalize on the capacity of rubrics to make the inherently subjective more objective. For example, rubrics can be used to assess the combination of experiences and artifacts in a student portfolio. These often consist in part of products identified in required classes and related experiences throughout a course of study. Examples of related experiences include concurrent practicums, medical rotations, or business internships that are completed for programmatic credit.

An overriding programmatic rubric may include strands that address expected levels of performance on final products. Capstone products would include concrete products such as a senior project, master's thesis, or comprehensive examination and also final process-focused performances like a capstone internship or collaborative work experience. With or without the addition of headings and subheadings to organize a longer, more intricate rubric into sections, a rubric can encompass a mix of products and processes.

To summarize, criteria described in performance or product rubrics, and the strands that comprise them, must meet the follow requirements: they must be (1) essential to the performance or product production task, (2) attainable by the student(s) whose work is being assessed, and (3) reflective of observable, developmentally appropriate proficiency levels specific to each criterion. Summaries of how that plays out in the two primary types of rubrics—for performance tasks and for tangible products—are included in the key considerations for this chapter.

KEY CONSIDERATIONS: PERFORMANCE TASK
AND ARTIFACT/PRODUCT RUBRICS

Performance task rubrics are designed to aid in the assessment of student work that focuses on demonstration of a specific skill or set of skills. The focus can be formative or summative. Demonstration of skills results in desired outcomes that are observable but not static. Performance outcomes cannot be placed on a professor's desk or on public display in final, tangible, two- or three-dimensional form.

Concrete artifact/product rubrics are designed to aid in the assessment of student work that focuses on the development and construction of a specific, tangible product. Products can also be assessed while in formative progress or when summarily completed. While skill(s) will be needed to create the desired product, the outcome is static, two- or three-dimensional. Product outcomes can be placed on a professor's desk, viewed on display in a public setting, or submitted as an electronic file.

3

Categories of Rubrics

Analytic and Holistic

Just as there are two primary *kinds* of rubrics for each of the assessment tasks—performances/processes or products/artifacts—there are two *categories* of rubrics: analytic and holistic. With an analytic rubric, the whole performance or product is considered in terms of its individual component parts. Rubric scores are determined by designing strand cells with the individual criteria that most closely match the performance or product.

In the case of holistic rubrics, by contrast, the essential components are described with much larger brush strokes. The focus is on an overview or a descriptive summary of a combination of essential elements rather than on separate, individual elements. Rubric scores are determined by designing strand cells with a preponderance of evidence that most closely describes the product or performance.

ANALYTIC RUBRICS

An analytic rubric is designed to assess only one specific component per strand. Designing an analytic rubric requires that the performance or product be broken down into the individual component parts that are essential to the successful enactment of the performance or the successful development of the product. For example, when teaching an introductory course for a master's degree in teacher leadership, my students were required to produce a product that involved drafting a philosophy of teacher leadership. This document served as a baseline evaluation of their dispositions and beliefs in several areas essential to being an effective, experienced teacher. (Students revised and resubmitted their philosophies as the last project in their master's program, with new perspectives gained as a result of their program of study.)

Because it was to serve as a baseline document, the evaluation emphasis of the initial rubric was on addressing the necessary components rather than on specifying the content or quality of those components. This was the case in part because it seems inappropriate to tell students what to believe in terms of a philosophy statement.

It was also the case because of curiosity to see their entry-level working definitions of curriculum, the role of education in a democratic society, and leadership. The instructions were not intended to be at all prescriptive so that students would not fall into the trap of writing what they thought the instructor wanted to read rather than what they really believed. The description students received of the project expectations was as follows, with the key components that became the rubric strands in boldface:

> Philosophy of Teacher Leadership: Candidates will write a short essay (**4–5 DS pages, not counting APA-format cover page or references**), using a **well-edited APA format,** that reflects upon *personal beliefs* related to what students should learn (**curriculum**), the **role of education in today's society** (local and global perspectives), and what constitutes **teacher leadership** (including the mentoring and coaching of new teachers). Candidates should include an **autobiographical discussion** of **how these beliefs were shaped** and **how these beliefs are evident in their personal teaching practice.**

With this assignment description as a starting point, an analytic rubric was developed to describe the ideal level of attainment (in the far left column), and the possible points associated with a product wherein the key components were expressed in the rubric strands labeled down the left-hand side of the rubric. It could be argued that a pure analytic rubric would have addressed each of the criteria in the first strand on format specifications (number of pages, APA cover page, and organization of the paper) and in the second strand on components addressed (curriculum, role of education in society, and teacher leadership) by describing them on separate strands. In this case, mainly because it was their first written assignment in the program and because part of the purpose of the assignment was to elicit from students their own definitions of the three concepts to be addressed, all three components were addressed in one strand in both cases.

The challenge when collapsing potentially stand-alone rubric strands into one strand is to be sure that the collapsed criteria are similar enough to function as an individual analytic strand. The wording used to describe the various cell levels must also provide an easy means for you to score any possible combination of product outcomes involving more than one component. This was accomplished satisfactorily in the rubric found in table 3.1.

Table 3.1. Assessment Rubric: Philosophy of Teacher Leadership—Initial Document (20 Possible Points)

Component	0	1	2	3	4
Format Specifications	<4 or >5 pages, no APA cover page, or difficult to follow.	4–5 DS pages, APA cover page, but challenging to follow in places.	4–5 DS pages, a few errors in APA cover page, well organized.	4–5 DS pages, APA cover page, well organized.	4–5 DS pages, APA cover page, well organized with at least one reference or direct quote.
Components Addressed	Two or all components (curriculum, role of education in society, teacher leadership) missing or vague.	One of three components missing, vague, or little/no mention of mentoring and coaching.	All three components addressed with mention of mentoring and coaching.	Clear sections for all three components, mention of mentoring and coaching.	Clear sections for all three components, strong treatment of mentoring and coaching.
Autobiographical Discussion	Autobiographical discussion missing or insufficient to support how beliefs were shaped.	Beliefs about teaching and learning not addressed in autobiographical discussion.	General statements about how beliefs about education, teaching, or learning were shaped.	Specific examples of how beliefs about education were shaped.	Specific examples of how beliefs about teaching and learning were shaped.
Putting Beliefs into Practice	Discussion of beliefs or their implementation in practice is missing.	Discussion of beliefs or their implementation in practice is vague.	Discussion of beliefs and their implementation in practice is adequate.	Discussion of beliefs and their implementation in practice is clear.	Discussion of beliefs is supported by at least one reference; implementation in practice is clear.
Edited Copy in APA Format	>7 typo, APA, or mechanical errors.	6–7 typo, APA, or mechanical errors.	4–5 typo, APA, or mechanical errors.	2–3 typo, APA, or mechanical errors.	0–1 typo, APA, or mechanical errors.

HOLISTIC RUBRICS

A holistic rubric is designed to assess multiple components per strand. Designing a holistic rubric still requires that the performance or product be broken down into individual components. The difference lies in these components being grouped in combinations that permit related components to be considered together in one strand rather than focusing on and scoring each individual component in its own strand. With more than one component in a strand, a product or performance may be an exact match for each of those components, or it may be a match for the majority of the components in a particular strand, aligning with a *preponderance of the evidence.*

For example, the National Council for the Accreditation of Teacher Education (NCATE) has used holistic rubrics to describe the levels of performance expected of programs designed to provide initial teaching certification or advanced certification for teachers or school administrators (2008). Teams of trained Board of Examiners members evaluate reports submitted electronically several months in advance of an accreditation visit and conduct site visits to verify information gleaned from the reports and the standards-aligned electronic artifacts. Schools seeking national NCATE accreditation for their education units use sets of holistic rubrics to prepare their documentation and, ideally, to assist in the initial design and ongoing development of educator preparation programs.

The first professional standard addresses candidate knowledge, skills, and professional dispositions. There are seven strands that fall under this standard, the first of which, strand 1a, addresses content knowledge for teacher candidates, initial and advanced, as indicated in the rubric in table 3.2 (NCATE, 2008, p. 16).

The same strand components are assessed at each of the column levels: breadth of content knowledge; demonstration of knowledge aligned with professional, state, and institutional standards; how knowledge is demonstrated; percentage of program completers passing required state assessments; and depth of content knowledge. A primary challenge in the design of holistic rubrics is the need to address each component at each level despite the fact that the components are combined into criterion groups rather than being presented as specific criteria.

A corresponding challenge when designing and using holistic rubrics is to be sure that all components are considered at every level rather than "slipping through the cracks" in one or more of the columns. One way to be sure both challenges are overcome is to convert the holistic rubric to an analytic rubric, as was done in table 3.3.

So why use a holistic rubric and not the analytic option? The holistic rubric provides for leeway and flexibility. It permits an overall score to be given

Table 3.2.   NCATE Standard 1a—Content Knowledge for Teacher Candidates, Initial and Advanced

UNACCEPTABLE	ACCEPTABLE	TARGET
Teacher candidates have inadequate knowledge of content that they plan to teach and are unable to give examples of important principles and concepts delineated in professional, state, and institutional standards. Fewer than 80 percent of the unit's program completers pass the content examinations in states that require examinations for licensure. Candidates in advanced programs for teachers do not have an in-depth knowledge of the content that they teach.	Teacher candidates know the content that they plan to teach and can explain important principles and concepts delineated in professional, state, and institutional standards. Eighty percent or more of the unit's program completers pass the content examinations in states that require examinations for licensure. Candidates in advanced programs for teachers have an in-depth knowledge of the content that they teach.	Teacher candidates have in-depth knowledge of the content that they plan to teach as described in professional, state, and institutional standards. They demonstrate their knowledge through inquiry, critical analysis, and synthesis of the subject. All program completers pass the content examinations in states that require examinations for licensure. Candidates in advanced programs for teachers are recognized experts in the content that they teach.

based on a majority, or preponderance, of evidence. In the NCATE rubric example above, suppose that artifacts produced by the candidates (1) supported their command of in-depth knowledge; (2) demonstrated this through examples of inquiry, critical analysis, and synthesis of content as described in the standards; and (3) indicated that all program completers passed the required licensure examinations. However, if (4) the candidates in advanced programs, while highly competent, are by no means recognized as content area experts, the unit could still be scored at the target level because most, a majority, a preponderance, three out of four of the strands, met the requirements for that level. This is especially helpful in circumstances where more than one artifact or demonstration of skill may be considered evidence of satisfying requirements in a given strand. For example, when assembling a standards-based portfolio, candidates may organize the portfolio by standard but may have considerable leeway regarding what they choose to include as evidence that they have met those standards.

A holistic rubric is also a logical choice when the performances or artifacts of more than one student are to be considered simultaneously as a basis for

Table 3.3. NCATE Standard 1a Rubric Converted to Analytic Format

STRAND	UNACCEPTABLE	ACCEPTABLE	TARGET
Breadth of Content Knowledge	Teacher candidates have inadequate knowledge of content that they plan to teach.	Teacher candidates know the content that they plan to teach.	Teacher candidates have in-depth knowledge of the content that they plan to teach.
Professional, State, Institutional Standards Alignment	[Candidates] are unable to give examples of important principles and concepts delineated in professional, state, and institutional standards.	[Candidates] can explain important principles and concepts delineated in professional, state, and institutional standards.	[Candidates] demonstrate their knowledge through inquiry, critical analysis, and synthesis of the subjects as described in professional, state, and institutional standards.
Percentage of Program Completers Passing State Assessments	Fewer than 80 percent of the unit's program completers pass the content examinations in states that require examinations for licensure.	Eighty percent or more of the unit's program completers pass content examinations in states that require examinations for licensure.	All program completers pass the content examinations in states that require examinations for licensure.
Depth of Content Knowledge	Candidates in advanced programs for teachers do not have an in-depth knowledge of the content that they teach.	Candidates in advanced programs for teachers have an in-depth knowledge of the content that they teach.	Candidates in advanced programs for teachers are recognized experts in the content that they teach.

assigning a score. This is the case with the NCATE rubric, which focuses on the aggregate performance and ability to produce supporting artifacts of all candidates in one or more programs within a department, school, or college. The strand pertinent to pass rates on required licensure examinations is the most readily apparent example as it provides a percentage of candidates in the unit who have passed the content examinations in their respective subject areas. The other three strands evidence inherent leeway in that there are myriad options for providing criteria to show candidate strengths in the processes and products related to content knowledge.

The result is a holistic rubric that can support formative evaluation processes as well as assessment of final performances or products. The dual applicability of rubrics for informing progress as well as assessing final related outcomes is one of their many inherent strengths. This is the case for analytic or holistic rubrics. Kinds of assessment tasks for which either category of rubric is the better fit are outlined in the key considerations for this chapter.

KEY CONSIDERATIONS: WHEN ANALYTIC AND HOLISTIC RUBRICS BEST FIT THE ASSESSMENT TASK

Analytic rubrics fit the assessment task best when:

- Assessing one specific component, or a very limited number of related components, per strand.
- Individual component parts are essential to the performance or product.
- Ratings need to be given based on discrete, single-component cell scores.
- One specific type of artifact or performance is considered evidence of satisfying the requirements in a given strand.
- The performance or artifact of only one student or group of students at a time is to be considered as a basis for assigning a score in the strand. (There can be exceptions to this premise.)

Holistic rubrics fit the assessment task best when:

- Assessing multiple related components per strand.
- Individual components are considered as criterion groups.
- Ratings need to be given based on a majority of evidence.
- There is leeway regarding what artifact(s) or types of performances may be considered evidence of satisfying requirements in a given strand.
- The performances or artifacts of more than one student or group of students are to be considered as a basis for assigning a score in the strand. (There can be exceptions to this premise.)

REFERENCE

National Council for the Accreditation of Teacher Education (2008). NCATE unit standards. Retrieved from http://www.ncate.org/Standards/NCATEUnitStandards/UnitStandardsinEffect2008/tabid/476/Default.aspx.

II

DESIGNING RUBRIC ASSESSMENTS

Matching Tool to Task, or
When a Rubric Is Not the Best Option

Effective as rubrics can be, they are not the best option in every assessment situation. Attempting to force fit a rubric to a performance task can result in frustration for rubric designers and for their students—precisely what well-designed and well-implemented rubrics are intended to circumvent. When I first began using rubrics, every assessment opportunity I encountered appeared to be a perfect opportunity for using a rubric. I sure fit the old saying, "Now that she has a hammer, everything looks like a nail," to the point that some of my students—and colleagues—would probably have been less than opposed to the idea of using a hammer on me. Or perhaps on one of my many rubrics.

Continuing the tool analogy, assessment tools need to fit the assessment tasks at hand. Using the correct tool can make the task easier. Using an inadequate or mismatched tool makes assessment tasks onerous, frustrating, and simply more work than they need to be. The kinds of assessment tasks mentioned in this chapter lend better to assessment-instrument options other than rubrics. Several will be considered, beginning with those where more limited variables are involved and moving to assessment tasks that are less prescriptive.

DICHOTOMOUS COMPONENTS

When the goal of an assessment task is to determine whether or not components on a list of criteria are present, it essentially generates a set of dichotomous component questions. A very simple nonacademic example would be a grocery list. As a shopper progresses through the store, he or she checks off each item placed in the shopping cart, indicating that it is present and has been selected for purchase. No check mark means the item is either not in the cart, has not been located, or is no longer wanted. Quality issues are not involved for purposes of the shopping list. It's a yes-or-no determination. As an academic example, if an instructor is evaluating a piece of written work solely in terms of whether or not a specific component was included but is not assessing the quality of that component, a simple checklist would serve the purpose much better than a rubric.

Rubrics are designed to help clarify and make observable that which is inherently subjective. In cases involving dichotomous, yes-no, present-absent, correct-incorrect, true-false component variables, there is little if any room for subjectivity. The criterion you want to see is either there or it is not. There is no in-between, and the dichotomous options are perfectly clear.

As another example, let's say that you are assessing whether or not an appropriately designed cover page has been used when submitting a paper, whether or not pagination has been included in that paper, and whether or not the references at the back of the paper are in the proper format. If your students are to the point where they can reasonably be expected to know what an appropriate cover page looks like, how to paginate, and how to design a bibliography or list of references, there are no developmental levels to be considered. There are only two performance levels to consider. You are not assessing quality issues regarding the assessment tasks, you are assessing whether or not a given criterion is present. On the one hand—written product components are in place and accurate. On the other hand—they are not. For this task, it would be more efficient to use a checklist rather than a rubric. Your record keeping could involve a simple two-column table with student names in the first column and the performance criteria labeled in columns to the right. If your students demonstrate the required criterion, a check or plus sign goes in the box; if they don't, it is left blank or a minus sign is used as in table 4.1.

The same markings could be provided to the student in matrix form. Another means of scoring the student's work, if each of the above components was worth two points, would be to provide points earned and a total score for each student. For example, Student #1 would receive the score of 2 + 0 + 2 = 4.

Table 4.1. Dichotomous Criterion Checklist—Written Product Components

Name	Cover Page	Pagination	Reference List/Bibliography
Student #1	+	−	+
Student #2	+	+	+
Student #3	−	+	+
Student #4	+	+	−

There are circumstances in which a dichotomous criterion is only one of many criteria to be assessed in a performance task. For example, you may be assessing the presence of an appropriately designed cover page along with several more complex components in a paper. In a circumstance like this you may want to include the dichotomous task in a comprehensive rubric to avoid the inconvenience of using more than one assessment instrument. It is possible to fit a dichotomous component or two into the design of a comprehensive rubric by using arrows to indicate that there is no "middle ground" for this particular strand, as indicated in table 4.2.

MODIFIED DICHOTOMOUS COMPONENTS

There may also be times when an individual criterion you want to include in a comprehensive rubric is a modified dichotomous component. In other words, it is clear when the component is missing, but there is room for a limited number of performance levels if the component is present, rather than being a clear-cut case of present or not. In cases like this a similar kind of modified dichotomous rubric strand design can be used, as shown in table 4.3.

OPEN-ENDED MODIFIED DICHOTOMOUS COMPONENTS

Another kind of modified dichotomous component appears in cases where (1) assessment of specific pieces of theoretical knowledge, applied knowledge, or skill demonstration, is the goal; (2) there is only one correct response to assessment items; but (3) optional responses are not offered from which to select a correct response. Instructors have historically referred to this as a "short answer" question. For example, a student may be required to write the chemical formulae for a set of common medications, name several poets who wrote in the nineteenth century, or provide the names of capital cities for a list of countries. The information provided in a student response is either correct or incorrect and a rubric would serve no purpose. Again, a simple dichotomous checklist or an all-or-nothing system of assigning points for correct answers would be used.

If, however, each response is worth more than one point and some responses are "more correct" than others, a rubric may be used to help an instructor objectively apply the same scoring criteria to each student's responses. In the following example, the instructor of a hypothetical undergraduate geography course has given a short pretest to assess some of the students' basic knowledge upon entering the course. Students were told that the

Table 4.2. Assessment Rubric—Philosophy of Leadership, Draft (20 Possible Points)

Component	0	1	2	3	4
Cover Page	No cover page or format contains errors.	←		→	Cover page, correct format
Format Specifications	<4 or >5 pages, or difficult to follow.	4–5 DS pages, but challenging to follow in places.	4–5 DS pages, well organized. ← →	4–5 DS pages, well organized, with at least one reference or direct quote.	4–5 DS pages, well organized, with at least three references or direct quotes.
Autobiographical Discussion	Autobiographical discussion missing or insufficient to support how beliefs were shaped.	Beliefs regarding teaching and learning not addressed in autobiographical discussion.	General statements about how beliefs about education, teaching, or learning were shaped.	Specific examples of how beliefs about education were shaped.	Specific examples of how beliefs about teaching and learning were shaped.
Putting Beliefs into Practice	Discussion of beliefs or their implementation in practice is missing.	Discussion of beliefs or their implementation in practice is vague.	Discussion of beliefs and their implementation in practice is adequate.	Beliefs and their implementation in practice are clear.	Beliefs supported by at least one reference; implementation in practice clear.
Edited Copy	>7 typos or mechanical errors.	6–7 typos or mechanical errors.	4–5 typos or mechanical errors.	2–3 typos or mechanical errors.	0–1 typo or mechanical error.

Table 4.3. Twenty-first-Century Curriculum Revisioning Project (28 Possible Points)

Component	0	1	2	3	4
Selected Curriculum	Curriculum is not a state or national professional org. curriculum	↓	↑	Curriculum is a proposed state or national professional org. curriculum	Curriculum is an approved state or national professional org. curriculum
Proposal Aligned with at Least One Standard	Not twenty-first-century standard(s) aligned	Indirectly twenty-first-century standard(s) aligned	Aligned with at least one twenty-first-century standard	Clearly aligned with at least one twenty-first-century standard	Clearly aligned with at least two twenty-first-century standards
Proposed Curricular Revision	Revision is hypothetical only	Specific site of implementation unclear	Single classroom only	More than one classroom but not whole grade level	Grade-level or school-wide
PowerPoint Slide Content	Missing one or more of the nine required components	One or more of the nine required components partially or vaguely addressed	All nine required components addressed	All nine required components professionally addressed	All nine required components clearly, thoroughly, professionally addressed
Informational, Persuasive PowerPoint Presentation	Problems with info, clarity, or pacing	Some unclear information	Clear, accurate presentation	Clear, accurate, well-paced, or persuasive presentation	Clear, accurate, well-paced, and persuasive presentation
Edited PowerPoint Copy	>7 typos or mechanical errors	6–7 typos or mechanical errors	4–5 typos or mechanical errors	2–3 typos or mechanical errors	0–1 typo or mechanical error
Contribution to Team Project*	Contributions inconsistent, late, poor quality, or provided in a negative manner	One of four contribution components are strong	Two of four contribution components are strong	Three of four contribution components are strong	Contributions are consistent, timely, high-quality, and provided in a positive manner

* Each team member will rate all group members' contributions. Instructor will average all scores to determine this rating.

Table 4.4.   Basic Entry-Level Knowledge—Geography 101

Assessment Task	1 point	2 points	3 points
Identify Capital Cities for a List of Countries	One or more cities identified were incorrect and not in the correct country	One or more cities identified were incorrect but in the correct country	All capital cities identified were correct
Place Major Rivers in Correct Country(s) on a World Map	One or more rivers placed in wrong country and location	One or more rivers placed in correct country, wrong location	All rivers placed in correct countries and locations
Label Countries on a Map of Africa	One or more country inaccurately labeled, with or without some labeled with a former name	One or more country labeled with a former name	All countries accurately labeled

test would be used solely to assess entry-level knowledge, results would not be factored into the final course grade, and the only way to earn zero points on any one of the three sections was not to attempt it. Students were not given any more information than that, which does violate a basic premise of rubric assessment, that students are to be provided with the rubric prior to their performance being assessed. This is not as essential in the case of a pretest on which scores are not used to determine the final point total for the course and are used solely to evaluate students' entry-level knowledge, as in table 4.4.

LIMITED RESPONSE COMPONENTS

Another common kind of assessment method or test question involves students selecting the correct response from several offered choices. This is commonly known as the multiple-choice question or, as we referred to it during my student days, the multiple-guess question. The latter label is a good indication of why this type of question may be falling out of favor as a staple of contemporary instructor-designed assessment instruments although it remains the mainstay of many electronically delivered examinations. Well-designed examination questions of this or any kind are intended to provide a means to assess students' knowledge rather than their ability to demonstrate standardized test taking savvy or to intuit nuances of test item interpretation.

Even when multiple-choice questions are well designed, there is a primary concern associated with this kind of assessment question. It forces the mindset of "one correct answer" without needing to self-generate the answer, which often runs counter to the kinds of analytical thinking needed to consider the myriad alternatives so often required in complex twenty-first-century environments. However, in instances where selecting the one correct answer from several options is an essential skill, the multiple-choice question remains a viable option. A rubric would serve no purpose in scoring assessments composed of multiple-choice questions unless some of the multiple choices are "more correct or less correct" than others. In such cases, a rubric may serve to clarify the relative accuracy of several possible responses to aid in teaching a process of analyzing potential responses in order to arrive at the most correct response.

The example in table 4.5 is drawn from the Educational Testing Service's (ETS) Sentence Equivalence questions, one of three new kinds of test questions designed to assess context-based verbal reasoning on the Graduate Record Examination (GRE) (found at http://www.ets.org/gre/revised_general/prepare/verbal_reasoning/sentence_equivalence/sample_questions). Test takers are asked to "Select the *two* answer choices that, when used to complete the sentence, fit the meaning of the sentence as a whole *and* produce completed sentences that are alike in meaning." So the first sentence must be completed in two ways to produce two sentences that mean essentially the same thing.

It would appear much more efficient to provide an answer key and talk through the reasons for the correct responses in class if an assessment of this nature is used. However, a rubric strand could be designed to specify levels of correct and incorrect reasoning to arrive at the answers as indicated in table 4.6. In this example, point totals are not assigned to the columns because all but the response pair in the far right column is incorrect. A rubric format is used only to provide a visual comparison of potential responses. The middle

Table 4.5.   GRE Sample Question

Although it does contain some pioneering ideas, one would hardly characterize the work as _____.

The multiple choices provided are (A) orthodox, (B) eccentric, (C) original, (D) trifling, (E) conventional, (F) innovative. The correct choices are C and F.

The accompanying explanation states that, "The word 'Although' is a crucial signpost here. The work contains some pioneering ideas, but apparently it is not overall a pioneering work. Thus the two words that could fill the blank appropriately are 'original' and 'innovative.' Note that 'orthodox' and 'conventional' are two words that are very similar in meaning, but neither one completes the sentence sensibly."

Table 4.6.   Analysis of Potential Responses, Sample 1, GRE Sentence Equivalence

Relative Accuracy of Selected Response	Completion words dissimilar in meaning and neither completes the sentence sensibly.	Completion words similar in meaning; neither completes the sentence sensibly.	Completion words dissimilar in meaning; one completes the sentence sensibly.	Completion words similar in meaning and complete the sentence sensibly.
Question 1	Any pairing of (A) orthodox or (E) conventional with (B) eccentric or (D) trifling	(A) orthodox and (E) conventional	(C) original or (F) innovative paired with (A) orthodox (B) eccentric (D) trifling or (E) conventional	(C) original and (F) innovative

column could be exchanged with the column second from the right if similarity of meaning for the two completion words is deemed to be more important than completing the sentence with at least one word that results in a sensible meaning for the sentence.

GENERATED LIST COMPONENTS

In another form of performance task, students are required to generate a list of components rather than respond to questions. An economics student may be asked to generate a list of international and multilateral financial institutions, a music student may need to draft a list of musical compositions from a specific time period or written in rondo form, graduate research students may be challenged to collaborate on a list of researchable topics. Students may be requested to place the resulting list in chronological or another rank order, using an instructor-determined ranking system or devising one of their own. However, if the individual items on the resulting list will not be evaluated in terms of objectively determined quality, a rubric would be irrelevant to the performance task.

This is also the case when quality descriptors are generated by the assessment process itself rather than provided as a component of the assessment instrument. Simple examples would be a pro-con list or a plus-delta chart. Although this may appear to be a case of dichotomous components, the criteria are determined by the students to be evaluated and will involve lists of multiple paired or unpaired variables. So despite the dual categorization, the focus of the assessment exercise remains that of compiling a list.

OPEN-ENDED RESPONSES

In some circumstances, any kind of forced choice is too confining to meet the intended purposes of the assessment process. This is the case when there is no one right answer being sought, desired responses often become more narrative in substance, and content may involve inherent elements of subjectivity. In such instances, an instrument to guide written responses, such as the matrix in table 4.7, may be more practical than a rubric. Assessing the depth of self-reflection or the mechanics of the written narrative may be aided by a

Table 4.7.   Capstone Practicum Assessment: Demonstration of Standards-Aligned Teaching Performance

NC#	Performance Component—We will:	Greatest Success(es)	Greatest Challenge(s)	What Was Learned
I-a	Encourage students to take responsibility for learning. Use classroom assessment data to inform program planning. Encourage students to foster safe environments.			
I-b	Collaborate to improve quality of learning.			
I-c	Collaborate to facilitate growth and decision making.			
I-d	Implement initiatives to improve education.			
I-e	Demonstrate ethical, professional collaborative practices.			
II-a	Provide nurturing, positive learning environments for students.			
II-b	Integrate culturally sensitive materials and ideas. Capitalize on diversity as a classroom asset.			
II-c	Help students hold high self- and peer expectations.			
II-d	Adapt instruction for students with special needs.			
II-e	Promote trust and understanding in the school community.			

rubric. However, when personalized, student-specific subjective information is the solicited outcome, the only way not to meet performance expectations is not to complete the assignment or not to do so in a manner commensurate with what is expected of students at that level. As is the case with most performance tasks, examples of work completed in a manner that meets expectations would be helpful for students.

STUDENT ABILITY TO SELF-ASSESS

I believe that one of the important elements of assessment, especially at the college or university level, is that of encouraging student self-assessment. This practice is encouraged, if not required, by national discipline-specific accrediting organizations but also makes sense because it is commensurate with good teaching.

One of the visual tools I've used to explain the purpose of self-assessment to students has been an adapted version of the Johari Window. Developed in the 1950s by Joseph Luft and Harry Ingham (thus the *Jo-Har-I* label), the window was originally used to teach communication skills. The simple two-by-two cell design can also be used to depict an individual's skill development level as it pertains to any given competency, as indicated by the matrix in table 4.8.

In terms of the four possible combinations of skilled or unskilled status and conscious or unconscious self-awareness of that status, Unconsciously Unskilled students who "don't know what they don't know" tend to be at the greatest disadvantage. They also tend to be challenging, if not dangerous, in field settings for their professors. There is an old saying by the Greek philosopher Epictetus that "A man [or woman] cannot learn what [s]he thinks

Table 4.8.   Self-Perceived Skill-Level Matrix

Consciously	Skilled	Unskilled
	Consciously Skilled	Consciously Unskilled
	Unconsciously Skilled	Unconsciously Unskilled
Unconsciously		

[s]he already knows." Students in this category will often get in the way of their own learning until they gain the insight to recognize their lack of skill. The objectivity of a rubric can be a starting point in helping students become aware of the progress yet to be made.

The group of students who fall into that Consciously Unskilled quadrant often feel they are at the greatest disadvantage, but in terms of potential they are not. They are at a point in their learning process where a well-designed rubric can assist with goal setting. Once students are aware they are not yet skilled, they can ascertain what it will take to develop the desired skills and begin the journey down that road.

In some ways, that is a more comfortable place to be than Unconsciously Skilled. I think some of my interns came to dread my inevitable question in field settings of "Why did that work?" Especially in the beginning weeks of the internship, this question often elicited a response along the lines of "I . . . am not really sure." Part of the job of a clinical supervisor in an internship experience is to help interns deconstruct successful as well as less-than-successful experiences. The specificity of analytic rubrics can be extremely helpful in this process.

Once students get to the point where they know the theoretical basis for their successes, and why techniques work or do not work in a given context, they are well on the way to being able to self-assess. At this point, they usually find themselves in the top left quadrant of Consciously Skilled and would be well positioned to extend existing rubrics or develop their own to assist in their ongoing acquisition of knowledge and skills.

SELF-ASSESSMENT AND
CONTENT-SPECIFIC COURSE EVALUATIONS

Most if not all colleges or universities have generic systems in place so that students can assess their courses and their professors. No, I am not going to use this as an example of inherent subjectivity, although many of my colleagues, especially if tenured or asked "off the record," credit these systems with being one of the factors that facilitate grade inflation. They can also be professionally destructive in the hands of politically motivated senior faculty or in the hands of anyone who simply doesn't know what they are looking at. One of the inherent weaknesses of such systems is that they assess all courses across the institution using the same criteria. That may provide a common ground for assessment of basic teaching competence in terms of inputs such as components of a well-designed syllabus, instructor accessibility to students, and yes, perceived fairness of the grading system.

What these systems are often not designed to consider is outputs in the form of student achievement. I am not referring to the letter grade that ultimately appears on a transcript but rather to what has been learned. Going back for a moment to my enlightening encounter with the Allegory of the Cave in chapter 1, I am referring to how well students perceive they have moved from point *a* to point *b* in regard to knowledge or skills acquired.

To gain insight into my students' perceptions of their growth, I designed a standards-based assessment instrument that I ask them to complete at the middle and end of semester-long courses. It has been referred to as a rubric but not by the author because it isn't. It is a Likert scale in a matrix, which all too often passes for a rubric despite the absence of specific, observable cell descriptions to define skill levels. In this case, the subjectivity of students being able to determine for themselves what "beginning skill" or "intermediate skill" means is permissible because it will differ for every student. Readers are welcome to insert their own professional standards and follow the process described below. The example of a completed standards-based assessment instrument, found in table 4.9, is drawn from my own e-file of assessments from classes previously taught. To analyze the skill-level responses for each of these ten standards-aligned components, two things were done:

1. For each skill area, I counted the number of candidates who indicated they had possessed each skill level before taking the course (the Roman-type numbers) and after taking the course (the italic numbers). Skill areas one, six, and seven had the greatest number of candidates indicating they were "not yet skilled" upon entry into the course. Skill areas four and five had the least number of students indicating they were not yet skilled, which was understandable because candidates in this course were experienced teachers who would be expected to "understand and respect" student differences.

2. For each skill area I also mapped the number of candidates for every possible pre/post combination, assigning 1 point for each skill level they attained above their baseline skill level. No points were given if a candidate indicated they remained at the same levels. (No students regressed.) For example, in the first skill area, six candidates started at the "not yet skilled" level and moved to "working toward beginning skill" by the end of the course. Seven started as "not yet skilled" and indicated that they felt they had progressed to "beginning skill" by the end of the class. All possible combinations for what I termed the "increase score" for all ten skill areas were tallied and analyzed.

The areas that showed the largest increase in skill levels were skill areas seven, six, and one. All three of these areas were the same three that had the highest number of students indicating they felt "not yet skilled" at all upon entry into the course. While this would mean these areas had the greatest potential for growth, it also means these were the most crucial areas in which growth was needed. Being able to accomplish this, with only one student indicating a level of "not yet skilled" in areas six and seven upon completion of the course, indicates candidate accomplishment in three complex skill areas of high importance to leaders in the profession and to success in a graduate program: (1) incorporating findings from educational literature into implications for field-based applications (transferring theory into practice); (6) critically reading and applying historical and contemporary professional literature such as theoretical, philosophical, and research-based material; and (7) analyzing and articulating connections between theory or philosophy, research findings, and their own current practice.

Yes, the one student who did not feel there was an improvement in his or her (the matrices may be submitted anonymously) skill level concerned me. The example in table 4.9 represented end-of-course data. It was because of this student's self-assessment scores that I encourage conducting an abbreviated version of this skill-level assessment at the midterm point.

In summary, there are instances in which a rubric is not a viable option or may simply not be the best assessment choice. When dealing with assessments consisting predominantly of modified or simple dichotomous components, limited response questions, generated lists, or open-ended questions where no particular response is considered correct or incorrect, assessment instruments such as simple checklists or charts may be more useful for tracking and scoring student work.

If rubrics are used at all in these instances, their function is best limited to that of clarifying expectations and teaching processes of reasoning rather than that of providing scores that will be factored into a final project or course grade. A sequential list of questions to be used in order to determine whether or not a rubric would be a good fit for a specific assessment task is provided in the key considerations for this chapter.

Table 4.9.   Course # Standards-Aligned Skills Assessment

Please rate your skill level when you entered _____ course # _____ on _____ date_ by placing a check (or X) in the appropriate box on the skill matrix below. Rate your skill level now, having almost completed _____ course # _____, by placing a plus sign in the appropriate box on the skill matrix. (Place the check and the plus in the same box if you believe your skill level has not changed.)

NC Advanced Teaching Standards-Aligned Skills	Not Yet Skilled	Working Toward Beginning Skill	Beginning Skill	Intermediate Skill	Increase Score
1. Incorporate findings from educational literature into implications for school and classroom applications.	**13**	5	1	1	
	–	6	11	3	**27**
2. Connect subject matter and issues addressed in this course to students' diverse needs in the context of school settings.	6	10	3	1	
		3	11	6	24
3. Seek, evaluate, and plan whether or not to implement pedagogical practices (for example, constructivism) for subjects taught within the context of a school setting.	8	4	5	3	
	–	5	7	8	20
4. Increase understanding of and respect for differences in students, including students with exceptionalities.	2	4	10	4	
	–	2	3	15	17
5. Understand and respect differences in the learning behaviors and outcomes expected in diverse communities.	3	7	6	4	
	–	3	8	9	15

6. Critically read and apply historical and contemporary educational literature, including theoretical, philosophical, and research materials.	15	2	3	0	
	1	*6*	*8*	*5*	*29*
7. Analyze and articulate connections between theory or philosophy, research findings, and current classroom practice.	16	3	1	0	
	1	*5*	*10*	*4*	*32*
8. Be able to identify and understand current knowledge and trends in education.	3	14	2	1	
	–	*3*	*11*	*6*	*22*
9. Engage in professional inquiry through reading, dialogue, reflection, professional development, and action research.	8	11	–	1	
	–	*4*	*14*	*2*	*24*
10. Participate in collaboration to explore and address educational problems.	3	14	3	–	
	–	*3*	*10*	*7*	*24*

Key: Ratings at point of entry are entered in roman tyoe; ratings at point of course completion are entered in italic type.

Chapter 4

KEY CONSIDERATIONS: QUESTIONS TO
DETERMINE IF A RUBRIC IS A VIABLE ASSESSMENT OPTION

1. Has a clearly visible product or performance process been identified? If YES:
2. Are you assessing mostly simple or modified dichotomous components? If NO:
3. Are variables expressed in limited response questions with one correct answer expected? If NO:
4. Are you evaluating a generated list whether ranked or unranked? If NO:
5. Are you evaluating open-ended responses with no one correct answer? If NO:
6. Is an element of subjectivity permissible? If NO:
7. Are you assessing the demonstration of a specific skill or set of skills, or the production of a tangible product? If YES: a rubric may be a viable assessment option.

5

Rubric Design

Analytic Rubrics

In this chapter, the ten steps of rubric design will be introduced using a performance example that will be familiar to most readers. This will be, at least in part, a print narrative version of a process that has been used to present the basics of rubric assessment to undergraduate or graduate students. Many of them approached the class sessions in which rubric assessment would be addressed with varying degrees of ennui. After all, they had seen rubrics before and could tell 'em when they see 'em. They had also made up their minds whether they liked them or disliked them based on the rubrics they had already encountered and how they were used or misused.

Former students had been promised that the session on rubrics would be "tasteful" and nonboring. If they didn't learn anything new in the first half of the class, they were welcome to skip the second half. The same promise holds true for the reader. This chapter will be "tasteful" (if not tasty) and nonboring. If something new is not learned by the start of the fifth step of analytic rubric design, skip the rest of this chapter and go on to chapter 6. A word of warning though: maybe the author's students were just being polite—nope, not likely, as they were overscheduled undergrads and tired graduate students taking three-hour evening classes—but a student has never bailed out at the halfway point.

DESIGNING AN ANALYTIC RUBRIC

The working example in this chapter is a nonacademic example, and readers will need to assemble some materials—or imagine they are assembled—to fully experience said example. Unless this chapter is being read well before noon, the reader is on a strict diet, or is one of the few people who truly hates what is about to be discussed, the real items will be preferred to the imagined versions. Put the book down and go get, purchase, or purloin whatever is needed to construct the perfect ice cream sundae.

No, this is not a joke. Yes, this will have something to do with rubrics. Now get thee to a kitchen or grocery store or both. To make the process more fun and more "real world" (as in rubric-design-by-committee), take along a small group of family, friends, or students. This will only be helpful if they agree to participate in the rubric-building phase of the experience too, not just in the sundae-consumption phase.

Step 1. All set? Good. Just so we all get the scoop, so to speak, the assessment task before us is to describe the perfect ice cream sundae. Although some assembly—that is, some process—is obviously required, a final product will be assessed rather than a performance process. There may be instances where both product and process are assessed in the same set of rubrics, but individual rubrics usually assess one or the other.

Step 2. The next step involves asking the key question: Is a rubric an effective, efficient option for this assessment purpose? Well—has a product or process been clearly identified? Yes: check. Are we dealing with simple or modified dichotomous components? No—there are myriad options available here. Walk into any commercial establishment that specializes in ice cream sundaes if verification is needed. Are the variables expressed in terms of limited response questions with a set of possible responses provided and one correct answer expected? Or how about limited response questions with no possible responses provided and one correct answer expected? No and no. A generated list whether ranked or unranked? Also negative. Open-ended responses with no one correct answer? Not unless the respondent is anti–ice cream, missing the sense of taste—or missing the sense of frivolity not usually associated with reading an academic book. So, therefore, is a rubric a viable option for this assessment task? Yes.

Step 3. Having decided that a rubric can and will be used to help describe the relative levels of excellence contributing to the perfect ice cream sundae, should this be done with a holistic or an analytic rubric? The underlying question is this: Would focusing on one specific component per strand (analytic rubric) or multiple components per strand (holistic rubric) better serve the purposes of the assessment task?

Probably a focus on specific components per strand, using an analytic design, would be the best bet for describing the components of the perfect ice cream sundae. The separate components can be identified, and there are not so many that the analytic approach to the assessment task would become unmanageable. In addition, the resulting rubric will be able to be used multiple times to assess individual products, in this case potentially many ice cream sundaes. Just as a check-and-balance procedure, however, the completed analytic rubric will be converted to a holistic rubric for comparison purposes later on in this chapter.

Step 4. Now the bulk of the work begins. Take a blank 8.5 x 11-inch piece of paper or open a new blank document on a laptop or electronic word processing gadget of choice. Draft a table with five columns and, for now, ten rows. Rows can always be deleted if you find they are not needed. This will result in a rubric template as in table 5.1, with four columns for value descriptors and one column, the one on the far left, for strand components.

Why use four columns for descriptors? The rubric could have been designed with three or five columns as well. (Two would be too few because it would result in a de facto dichotomous checklist.) Three-column rubrics work well for assessment tasks without much need to show increments of developmental continuity. They are also a good match for assessment tasks when components of products or performances are readily identifiable as good, bad, or somewhere in between.

The author has been a traditional fan of the five-column rubric because it permits designers to identify some middle ground. That being said, sometimes the middle ground provides an easy out, an opportunity to straddle the fence when making an assessment decision. With a four-column rubric, room is provided for developmental variation. However, with an even number of columns, the assessor needs to come down on one side or the other of the good or not-so-good midpoint.

Another common addition is a column for a score of zero to account for the possibility of components being omitted completely or present in such basic or poorly demonstrated form they do not yet merit rubric points. Designing a column for "zero" to be the fifth column in a five-column rubric can provide a

Table 5.1. A Basic Analytic Rubric Template

	Descriptor	*Descriptor*	*Descriptor*	*Descriptor*
Component				
Component				
Component				
Component				
Component				
Component				
Component				
Component				
Component				

good compromise when a design team is having difficulty choosing between a four-column or five-column rubric.

Examples of rubrics that use more than five column levels are rather uncommon. If a rubric is composed of more than five columns, it usually addresses performance tasks that span multiple years and several developmental phases in students' professional training.

The most practical suggestion regarding how to determine the appropriate number of columns is to make your best guess and begin drafting the rubric. If trouble is encountered while devising language for one of the columns *and* everything that needs to be assessed is being addressed in the columns that have been completed, omit a column. If too much information is being forced into one of the existing columns, try inserting an additional column.

Going back to step four, title the top of the far left column "Components." Decide upon the component criteria to be assessed: the components of an ice cream sundae. Do not be surprised if this is not as easy as anticipated. It may generate some debate if a collaborative process is being attempted. Working toward consensus or compromise may be necessary if you are not drafting the rubric on your own. Add a title for the rubric while you are at it. When this has been done with a class, the result has typically been something like the initial rubric draft in table 5.2.

The reader's rubric-in-progress may look a bit different because different elements may have been identified as vital to the perfect ice cream sundae or may have been named differently. Please work with what you have drafted and do not change it to conform to the hypothetical example provided. (Delete any remaining blank rows. They can always be re-added if needed.) Some of the elements included in the example may have been omitted from yours and that is ok too.

For example, this author fully believes that the perfect sundae is the classic turtle sundae, which consists simply of three scoops of vanilla ice cream, hot fudge sauce, caramel sauce, whole roasted and slightly salted pecans, optional dairy whipped cream, and a cherry. This exquisite concoction is ever

Table 5.2.   Rubric Sample: The Perfect Ice Cream Sundae

Components
Whipped topping
Fruit topping
Crunchy topping
Sauce/pourable topping
Ice cream
Container

so flawlessly executed by Kopp's Frozen Custard in Milwaukee, Wisconsin. (No, they are not paying the author for this endorsement. However, if they'd like to, the author would be an amenable spokesperson—provided the compensation were to be in kind.) However, other sundae consumers may not reach sundae nirvana unless the ice cream can hardly be seen under all the layers of toppings and sprinkles and fruit.

It is your prerogative, indeed your responsibility as the designer of a rubric, to set the criteria to be assessed and the levels of excellence to be met. In actual application, strand descriptors tend to be more specific contrasted with those in the example provided in table 5.2, which were purposely designed to be inclusive.

The "pourable topping" descriptor could mean anything from chocolate sauce to melted peanut butter. The "crunchy topping" category includes sprinkles, crushed nuts, seeds, toffee bits, cookie pieces, and so on. Fruit topping could include strawberries or pineapple, apple chunks or banana slices. Whipped topping could include everything from dairy whipped cream to a frothy gelatinous mix in a fruit flavor. (If it was initially decided not to construct a sundae but only to read about it, are you getting hungry and changing your mind yet?)

In addition to degree of specificity, considerations regarding quality or quantity need to be addressed. In some rubric strands, the cell descriptors are actually quantity-structured and focus on "more is better," or perhaps in the case of some types of error, "less is better." A variation on that theme takes an additive approach, starting with a basic skill or demonstrated competency and showing how its enactment becomes more sophisticated as it is developed across the span of the rubric strand. (Additive rubric strands are discussed in chapter 7.)

Given that this rubric is about food, each of the strands could be subdivided into a section addressing quantity as well as a section pertaining to quality. In our example, the quantity-quality issue was circumvented by the disclaimer (note) at the bottom of the rubric, which stated the deliberate choice to avoid issues pertaining to quantity and address only those of quality (see table 5.6 later on).

As the reader may have observed by this point, the entire process of rubric design, with its many considerations, is challenging enough when undertaken independently. When it is collaboratively undertaken, and there are multiple designers with their figurative or literal hands on the rubric, the challenges of a task that would appear to be quite simple—identifying rubric strands—can quickly surface and compound.

For example, if the bottom element in our example rubric—the container—is omitted, the ice cream sundae comes apart. "Yes," a rubric designer might say, "but it doesn't really belong as a rubric strand because it is not part of the sundae, it is not edible." "Oh yeah?" a student, family member, or colleague may counter. "Well what if the container is a waffle bowl, how about that?"

And so the conversation/debate/argument begins. This is amusing when assessing an ice cream treat. It is much less so when assessing work that will be part of the basis for determining a course grade—or for that matter, for determining whether or not a student will be a candidate for a degree or a professional license.

When a course instructor designs a rubric strand or any other part of the rubric for purposes of course-related assessment, this debate is avoided. That in itself, however, is a two-sided coin because then the rubric designer's own thinking is not challenged. Any potential holes in the fabric of your rubric may not be readily identified until it is distributed to a classroom full of students. If there are discrepancies at this point, students will be only too willing to find them, whether or not they point them out to the instructor.

As has become a running refrain in this book, be sure whatever strands are identified can be easily understood. Rubric strands also need to fit every assessment task the rubric will be used to address, and there should not be any assessment tasks that will have unaddressed components. If a component is left unaddressed by conscious choice, that's fine. However, it diminishes the credibility of the rubric as an assessment tool if a key component goes unaddressed because a strand is accidentally left out of the rubric.

Step 5. The next step is easier than the former and involves providing the numerical ratings or other scoring system, if any is to be used, and selecting the column descriptors. Numerical ratings are necessary only if the rubric levels achieved will need to be converted into a numerical score for formative or summative assessment purposes of any kind.

Just for practice, let's say a national competition for the perfect ice cream sundae is underway and the rubric currently being designed might be used to help select the winner. In this case, numbers may be needed as column headings, so start by giving the best column a rating of 4 and working down from there. Include the resulting total number of possible points for the entire rubric beside the title of the rubric as in table 5.3.

Why not 0-1-2-3? Some designers of rubrics feel that a zero in a column is never appropriate and the only way a strand criterion can rate a zero is if it is omitted completely. When a column heading of zero is included, the language of the cells in the "zero" column can be crafted to align with omission of the element. There is no right or wrong answer in and of itself as far as the use of zero is concerned.

Whether or not a zero is included, the rating scale used for the column headings needs to fit the assessment structure and purpose. In this particular

Table 5.3. Rubric Sample: The Perfect Ice Cream Sundae (24 Possible Points)

Ratings:	1	2	3	4
Components:				
Whipped topping				
Fruit topping				
Crunchy topping				
Sauce/pourable topping				
Ice cream				
Container				

assessment example, no matter how badly the criteria in the rubric strands are represented, they will be present. Therefore, I chose to make a rating of 1 the lowest possible score rather than a zero.

Why not 4-3-2-1? Must rubrics be designed with the strongest elements on the right side of the rubric? No. This too is personal preference. Just be sure students understand the rating scale so they don't panic if they glance at a scored rubric and mentally juxtapose the scores.

For that matter, must the highest score be the best? Or can the score closest to a 1 *be* number one? It could—again, just about anything is possible if students understand the rating system and know what to expect. There are no numerical reasons why this could not work.

However, rating systems wherein the highest accumulation of points translates to the better grade are more frequently used. They are also easier to convert to letter-grade systems and to combine with point totals from other kinds of assessments in addition to rubrics when using multiple forms of assessment in the same course or semester. Finally, systems in which higher scores are assigned to better products or performances are usually more readily understood by students, including international students.

While scores for column headings are being addressed, what about the practice of providing a range of scores for each column, as in table 5.4? Some rubric designers claim this provides flexibility. Others believe it goes too far in the direction of making ratings subjective to the extent of raising concerns about equity and fairness. This is precisely the kind of issue rubrics are intended to prevent. If the same rubric cell description could be rated a 3 or a 4, how could the difference be defended except on the grounds of subjective

Table 5.4. Rubric Sample: The Perfect Ice Cream Sundae

Ratings:	1–2	3–4	5–6	7–8

criteria or subjectively applied criteria? This problem is only compounded if wider ranges of scores are assigned to column headings.

If rubric designers choose to do either in the name of flexibility, it is their right. However, they need to be aware that the resulting rubric scores are at least somewhat inherently subjective. They are also not as legally defensible as an assessment measure. This may be one reason some mainstream campus course assessment software does not provide the option of including a range of scores on rubric columns.

When designing rubrics, the column headings are often limited to a numerical score. However, if column descriptor terms are desired, this is the time to add them. Craft column headings that are positive, neutral, or nonpunitive in nature and that align with the numerical rating of the column. That is simple to do with the column on the far right; it just takes a little more thought as one moves toward the left.

When working with four-column or five-column rubrics, it is often helpful to consider the highest-value column an outlier. When this approach is taken, not many students should be expected to achieve this level. If they do, that's great, but top scores on all strands of all rubrics for class projects should not be an expectation for an A in a course.

This outlier column heading may be something like "exemplary," "outstanding," or "exceeds expectations." The next column in, the 3 column in the example, should be attainable by the solid A students in the class and some of the B students.

When four-level rubrics are used for the purpose of assessments associated with state licensing organizations or professional association key evidence portfolios, a 3 is the level of performance expected to demonstrate an acceptable level of competence. Examples of column headings would be "high quality," "excellent," or "competent."

The second column from the left in a four-column rubric is often the hardest to name. Work in this column may be assessed as work in progress, as coming along nicely but not quite there yet, or as just not cutting it. The latter mindset will produce column headings such as "struggling," "not yet achieving," or "meets minimal expectations." A more positive, work-in-progress approach would favor headings such as "developing," "approaching good quality," or "working to meet expectations."

The column on the far left, while clearly not a column where students want their work rated, needs to be clearly labeled yet respectful. Examples in common usage include "unsatisfactory," "needs improvement," and "does not yet meet expectations." With all of this in mind, these labels may be used for further developing the rubric in table 5.5.

This should go without saying, but as long as the issue has come up, this is being said anyway: When designing rubrics or any other form of assess-

Table 5.5. Rubric Sample: The Perfect Ice Cream Sundae (24 Possible Points)

Ratings:	1—Needs Improvement	2—Approaching Good Quality	3—High Quality	4—Outstanding
Components:				
Whipped topping				
Fruit topping				
Crunchy topping				
Sauce/pourable topping				
Ice cream				
Container				

ment, it is essential to use respectful language. The author recently saw a rubric strand where the criterion was something along the lines of "amount of support a student needed from the professor." This seemed a rather unusual criterion upon which to rate a student in the first place. The language in one of the cells in the left-hand column read "student is a parasite."

We all have moments of frustration or episodes of late-night humor, but this kind of demeaning terminology does not belong in an assessment rubric. (This rubric appeared in an article in a professional journal. Neither the source nor the profession is being identified here with the intent of not embarrassing the authors.)

This should also go without saying, but again it is being said anyway because these errors have been observed so often when rubrics are designed: It is essential to use correct spelling, capitalization, grammar, style mechanics, terminology, and punctuation when drafting rubric language. If any abbreviations are used, beyond the most common or basic, provide a key at the bottom of the rubric. If in doubt, err on the side of too much clarity and provide the key.

Every interaction with students—whether in person, on paper, or online—is an opportunity to model expected professional behavior. It is respectful as well as professionally responsible to provide print communication at the same level or better than what is expected from students. This is especially the case if the printed material is important enough to convey expectations for the assessment of course-related performances or products.

Step 6. This is the most challenging of the ten steps: writing the observable assessment criteria for each cell. Cells are composed of the intersections of criteria down the left margin rows with ratings across the top columns. Start with the outside columns and work your way in.

It is easy to describe a component at its best and at its worst. The areas in between are more difficult to define in just a few words. Remember to decide up front how any issues of quantity and quality will be addressed.

Omit all nonessential words. If you find the word *and* is being used a lot when working across a row, it may mean that these criteria will need to be split in two. Another row may be needed to accommodate more than one criterion. Work to maintain consistency in phrasing each of the cells in the strand while moving across the row.

Use language that focuses on the performance task or rubric strand component, not on the performer. One of the inherent strengths of a rubric is that it does just that, puts an objective focus on the work to be accomplished. Rubric usage can take some of the fuel away from the fires of perceived favoritism, "personality conflict," and gender or ethnic bias.

For example, there is a world of difference between a rubric cell that reads, "The student's paper was poorly written with more than seven APA errors," and a rubric cell that simply states, ">7 APA errors." One is punitive; the other states objective fact.

A small detail? "Semantics"? Perhaps. But the more objective versions tend to be easier to write and take up less space in a rubric cell. So whenever possible and practical, why not pull references to students out of the rubric language and focus on the work instead? The students will know the rubric is being used to assess their work without mention of their student status in the rubric cells.

Remember that "observable" is a key concept. "Student believes/feels/thinks" does not describe an observable behavior. However, what students do as a *result* of those beliefs, feelings, or thoughts can be described and can be observed.

Before looking at the example work for step six, try drafting the outside rubric columns. If this has not already been done, it seriously may help to literally or mentally construct an ice cream sundae at this point. Get some "hands on" experience, describe what is being tasted—or what the reader wishes were being tasted—and try drafting the far right column as the ice cream creation is being savored. When some language has been drafted, imagine the worst ice cream sundae ever experienced or heard about and take a run at the far left column. What one version of this would look like is in table 5.6.

Examine the consistency in phrasing from one column to the other. Does punctuation fall in the same or similar places? Are the same kinds of elements described, using consistent language to refer to them while moving across the columns in each strand? The author gave in to subjective commentary on the container strand (and, for that matter, on the footnote) but would not do this if it were a serious rubric to describe a student performance or product. It was only done because the rubric in the example is a lighthearted one being used to demonstrate the basic steps in rubric construction. Revise the working self-constructed draft as necessary. Feel free to borrow ideas or cells/rows from the rubric drafts provided.

Table 5.6.   Rubric Sample: The Perfect Ice Cream Sundae (24 Possible Points)

Ratings:	1 — Needs Improvement	2 — Approaching Good Quality	3 — High Quality	4 — Outstanding
Components:				
Whipped topping	Sour taste or runny, separating			Sweet, light, holds soft swirls
Fruit topping	Spoiled, moldy, or cloudy juice			Looks fresh cut; clear, sweet juice
Crunchy topping	Soggy, stale			Crisp, flavorful
Sauce/pourable topping	Tastes odd, not thick			Bold, sweet taste; thick
Ice cream	Gritty or freezer burned; odd taste			Smooth, silky; creamy taste
Container	Doesn't support the sundae— what a mess!			Supports and compliments the sundae— edible too!

Please note: Size of the sundae, whether one scoop or a quart, is purely an individual preference. This rubric focuses on quality aspects by intentional design, taking a gourmet rather than gourmand approach to this culinary topic and assessment process.

Ready to finish up? Try drafting the middle two columns. This will probably be more challenging than drafting the outer two columns. That's usually the case, even for experienced rubric designers. If it is found some of the language in the cells for the outer two columns needs to be revised when drafting the inner two columns, that's ok. It is not unusual. See what has been developed as a full draft and then compare and contrast it with the example in table 5.7. This completed rubric follows all of the steps and demonstrates all of the suggested pointers for rubric development.

Step 7. The seventh step would be to add headings within the rubric, if desired, to group the criteria for purposes of easier viewing or scoring. This is optional in the case of analytic rubrics but is often needed for holistic rubrics given the more inclusive, comprehensive nature of the cells. The ice cream rubric is compact enough that headings or subheadings are not necessary and would serve no organizational purpose.

Step 8. The eighth step provides rubric designers with a means for giving one or more of the strands or, if headings are used, one or more of the sections greater or lesser emphasis than the remaining strands or sections. This is often helpful when determining the composite score for the performance

Table 5.7.　Rubric Sample: The Perfect Ice Cream Sundae (24 Possible Points)

Ratings:	1—Needs Improvement	2—Approaching Good Quality	3—High Quality	4—Outstanding
Components:				
Whipped topping	Sour taste or runny, separating	Bland or loses shape quickly	Sweet; light, soft, droopy swirls	Sweet, light, holds soft swirls
Fruit topping	Spoiled, moldy, or cloudy juice	No longer fresh, tangy juice	Looks recently cut; clear, sweet juice	Looks fresh cut; clear, sweet juice
Crunchy topping	Soggy, stale	Getting soft, losing flavor	Almost crisp, good flavor	Crisp, flavorful
Sauce/ pourable topping	Tastes odd, not thick	Bland taste, lumpy	Sweet taste, smooth	Bold, sweet taste; thick and smooth
Ice cream	Gritty or freezer burned; odd taste	Uneven texture, adequate taste	Smooth, creamy taste	Smooth, silky; creamy dairy taste
Container	Doesn't support the sundae	Sundae is leaking through in a few places	Supports the sundae effectively	Supports and compliments the sundae— may be edible too!

Please note: Size of the sundae, whether one scoop or half a dozen, is purely an individual preference. This rubric focuses on quality aspects by intentional design, taking a gourmet rather than gourmand approach to this culinary topic and assessment process.

or product. This is done by assigning weightings, if desired. It may be easier to demonstrate than to explain.

In the example of the ice cream rubric as it exists in table 5.7, there are 24 possible points that can be earned. This is the case if every one of the six components is rated "outstanding" and therefore earns 4 points. To demonstrate the use of weightings, return to the hypothetical premise that the rubric is being used as part of a national competition to give an award for the perfect ice cream sundae.

Take that a step further by imagining that a company that is a national advocate of eating more ice cream is underwriting the competition. It is understandable that the hypothetical underwriter of this competition would want to put more emphasis on the ice cream component being adjudicated as part of the perfect sundae. To meet that assessment need, the designer or implementer of the rubric could choose to "weight the ice cream strand double."

This is indicated by placing "(x2)" in the component descriptor cell on the far left column of the rubric. Count whatever score that strand is awarded

Table 5.8. Rubric Sample: The Perfect Sundae Made with Ice Cream (24 Possible Points)

Ratings:	1—Needs Improvement	2—Approaching Good Quality	3—High Quality	4—Outstanding
Components:				
Whipped topping	Sour taste or runny, separating	Bland or loses shape quickly	Sweet; light, soft, droopy swirls	Sweet, light, holds soft swirls
Fruit topping	Spoiled, moldy, or cloudy juice	No longer fresh, tangy juice	Looks recently cut; clear, sweet juice	Looks fresh cut; clear, sweet juice
Crunchy topping	Soggy, stale	Getting soft, losing flavor	Almost crisp, good flavor	Crisp, flavorful
Sauce/ pourable topping	Tastes odd, not thick	Bland taste, lumpy	Sweet taste, smooth	Bold, sweet taste; thick and smooth
Ice cream (x2)	Gritty or freezer burned; odd taste	Uneven texture, adequate taste	Smooth, creamy taste	Smooth, silky; creamy dairy taste
Container	Doesn't support the sundae	Sundae is leaking through in a few places	Supports the sundae effectively	Supports and compliments the sundae— may be edible too!

Please note: Size of the sundae, whether one scoop or half a dozen, is purely an individual preference. This rubric focuses on quality aspects by intentional design, taking a gourmet rather than gourmand approach to this culinary topic and assessment process.

twice. This will increase the number of possible composite points that can be earned on the rubric to 28, as indicated in the revised version of the rubric in table 5.8.

It is also possible to deal with strand weights by making them worth only half of the default value by placing "(x.50)" in the strand descriptor cell. (See table 11.9 for an example.) Any ratio may be used for weighting purposes as long as it accurately represents the importance of the strand components to the overall product or performance. It must then be accurately factored into the scoring system for the rubric in which it is used.

Step 9. The ninth step involves piloting the finished rubric by using it to assess additional products—that is, additional ice cream sundaes. This can be done by the rubric designer or by anyone else enlisted to assist in this endeavor. Bribery may be effective here: the carrot of being able to design and/or devour an ice cream sundae may be well worth the stick of having to use the recently drafted rubric to assess it.

It may be found, as alluded to previously, that different people have different ideas about what criteria belong down the left-hand side of the rubric as well as what descriptive language belongs in the cells. That is to be expected. What readers want to find out from the piloting process is whether or not the rubric designed is applicable in every anticipated performance task assessment situation for which the rubric was developed.

Step 10. If it appears this is the case, based on piloting the rubric, take the tenth and final step. Move to full implementation and use the newly designed rubric for its intended purpose. If unanticipated gaps in applicability are found, despite a good-faith attempt to pilot the rubric, revise the rubric and keep revising it until the problems are solved.

Earlier in the chapter it was promised to provide a copy of the rubric in holistic form. This assessment rubric quite clearly belongs in the analytic realm for all the reasons stated in the third chapter, but look at the same rubric

Table 5.9.   Converting an Analytic to a Holistic Rubric: The Perfect Ice Cream Sundae

Ratings:	1 — Needs Improvement	2 — Approaching Good Quality	3 — High Quality	4 — Outstanding
Components: Whipped topping, Fruit topping, Crunchy topping Sauce, Ice cream, Container	Topping tastes sour; is runny, separating. Fruit spoiled or moldy, cloudy juice. Soggy, stale topping. Sauce tastes odd or spoiled. Ice cream is gritty or freezer burned, odd taste. Container doesn't support the sundae.	Topping tastes bland, loses shape quickly. Fruit no longer fresh, tangy juice. Topping getting soft, losing flavor. Sauce tastes bland is lumpy. Ice cream has uneven texture, adequate taste. Sundae is leaking through in a few places.	Topping is sweet; light, soft, droopy swirls. Fruit looks recently cut with clear, sweet juice. Topping almost crisp with good flavor. Sauce tastes sweet, is smooth. Ice cream smooth and creamy. Container supports the sundae effectively.	Topping is sweet, light, holds soft swirls. Fruit looks fresh cut with clear sweet juice. Topping crisp and flavorful. Sauce has bold, sweet taste; thick and smooth. Ice cream is smooth, silky, with creamy dairy taste. Container supports and compliments the sundae— may be edible too!

Please note: Size of the sundae, whether one scoop or half a dozen, is purely an individual preference. This rubric focuses on quality aspects by intentional design, taking a gourmet rather than gourmand approach to this culinary topic and assessment process.

in a holistic format to better understand why that is the case (see table 5.9). A simple direct-conversion holistic version of the analytic rubric could still work. However, it would take much longer to use, would not permit one of the individual strands to be weighted, and would involve a lot more deliberation to arrive at a final defensible score.

Before going on to the process of designing a holistic rubric in the next chapter, the steps followed for designing the analytic rubric will be summarized and reviewed. The ten steps for the development of an analytic rubric may be found in the key considerations for this chapter.

KEY CONSIDERATIONS:
THE 10 STEPS IN ANALYTIC RUBRIC DEVELOPMENT

Step 1:   Identify the goal of the assessment task and if it involves processes or products or both.

Step 2:   Be sure a rubric is an effective, efficient assessment option.

Step 3:   Determine if an analytic rubric is the best fit for your assessment task.

Step 4:   Determine the row/strand components to be assessed.

Step 5:   Select the number of columns and their descriptors and/or numerical ratings.

Step 6:   Draft the observable assessment criteria for each cell in every strand.

Step 7:   Decide whether or not headings would be helpful to organize the rubric.

Step 8:   Add weightings, if appropriate to augment column numerical ratings.

Step 9:   Pilot the rubric and revise as needed.

Step 10: Implement the rubric in practice.

6

Rubric Design

Holistic Rubrics

After an initial run at rubric design, enjoy the rest of that ice cream sundae while reading about another example of rubric construction. In the sundae simulation, work involved an assessment task wherein the components that composed the whole were quite well known.

Sometimes that is not the case. Not only must an instructor scope out the language for the rubric cells but he or she must also analyze performance task products in search of the specific individual criteria that make up the performance task. In simpler language, rubric assessment designers may not be 100 percent sure what they are looking for in terms of the components that compose a high-quality finished product or performance.

They know a good one when they see it, and they know a bad one when they see it. But they either have never stopped to analyze the individual components or have become so accustomed to performing the task well themselves that it is difficult to break it down into small increments for a beginner. Instead of taking an inductive approach to rubric construction, starting with well-known parts of a whole, it is possible to take a deductive approach and use whole finished products as a starting point from which to identify the parts.

In the case that comes to mind, a former colleague was experiencing frustration with the quality of written work that had been received from undergraduate students. They had been asked to write a five-page college-level essay on a topic appropriate to the course content. The resulting essays were "all over the map" in terms of quality. It was suggested that a rubric might provide guidance in the writing process, clarify what was expected, and provide a means to make what seemed overwhelming a more approachable assessment task. This would also eventually save the professor from writing the same comments on papers over and over again in the case of commonly made errors.

In this case, the colleague indicated that it was difficult to determine exactly what students were doing wrong. There also wasn't time to teach composition in addition to everything else that had to be covered during the semester. Rather than starting with an instructor-designed rubric, piloting the rubric, revising if needed, and then fully implementing the rubric, another approach had to be taken. A rubric would need to be designed based on the first round of student work submitted.

DESIGNING A HOLISTIC RUBRIC

Step 1. The assessment task was to evaluate a five-page undergraduate essay. As a starting point, the professor separated the most recent round of essays into four groups: those that had earned the grades of A, B, C, and D. The rubric designer wanted to find patterns of errors and also help clarify for students what was meant by the expectation of college-level writing. The piles of essays came in.

The resulting analysis process used was similar to what qualitative researchers might call a modified grounded theory approach. The process involved reading through the essays not in search of content themes but rather in search of trends pertaining to writing mechanics.

The task was approached by making a list of what was observed to be present, the characteristic criteria, of an A paper. Focus then moved on to the B pile, seeking especially to find how the same criteria identified in the A papers would be represented in the B papers. The same process was followed for the C and D papers, building the matrix that would become the basis for an assessment rubric.

Step 2. Is a rubric the most effective, efficient assessment option? Well, there was a clearly identified product. No simple or modified dichotomous components were involved, or at least not many of them. It was an essay to be assessed, not limited response questions, a generated list, or open-ended response questions. Besides, one of the initial uses for rubrics, after scoring visual art projects, was when the National Council of Teachers of English began encouraging their use for scoring K–12 student compositions decades ago. The initial criteria, combined with the fact that this was an assessment task involving a written composition, was a pretty good indicator that, yes, a rubric would be a viable assessment option.

Step 3. Do we want to use an analytic or a holistic rubric? The author confesses a bias toward analytic rubrics, at least as a starting point. Their use makes it harder for a component to be missed during the design process or when students are using a rubric to check their own work in progress. It is suggested that most rubrics be started as analytic rubrics. If it then makes better sense to group components or collapse several components into fewer strands based on the purpose of the rubric and its intended audience(s), it can be done. That is easier than to go the other way and separate components into more strands in an attempt to alleviate confusion.

Think of the matter of distributing components into strands with the same rationale that would be used when entering discrete numerical data into a statistical analysis program. If, for example, subjects' ages were entered as 20, 21, 21, 22, 25, 26, 27, 29, 30, and it was decided to sort the data by ranges of 20–22, 20–25, and 26–30, that could be done. But suppose a score of 5 had been entered under "age range of 20–25" without actually entering the raw score data for the individual ages. It would not be possible to go back and regroup the data if at a later time a researcher wanted to identify the actual ages of subjects between ages 20 and 22.

In like manner, starting with an analytic approach then going back and experimenting with grouping or collapsing the cells into a holistic rubric format is usually easy. It is much more difficult to start with a holistic approach and then attempt to convert it to an analytic rubric by disaggregating holistic criteria. It is not impossible; it is simply more time consuming and usually more difficult. So for now, start with an analytic rubric.

Step 4. Determine the criteria to be assessed. Based only on what was seen in the papers, there were many criteria that ended up down the left-side margin. These were originally listed as they were encountered, going back at a later time to arrange them under headings in alphabetical order.

Step 5. Determine the column descriptors and the numerical scores or other rating systems. In this case, step five had essentially been done. The rubric columns were labeled with the grades that had been assigned to the stacks of papers: A, B, C, and D.

Step 6. Determine the observable components for each intersection of criterion and rating. In most cases of rubric design, it is easiest to start with the column describing the best possible performance or product, go to the other extreme, then complete the columns in the middle. In this case, every cell in the D column was completed along with several in the C column, fewer in B, and even less in the A column. It had made more sense for this rubric design process to start with the column describing the essays with the lowest scores.

The task going in was to identify a pattern of errors associated with each grade level. Starting with the lowest level actually made this step if not easier at least more systematic. The next step was to scan the stacks of papers receiving higher scores to see how the same criteria had been represented in those papers.

Step 7. Group the criteria under headings. Arranging the criteria under headings is an optional step in the design of an analytic rubric. It is almost always essential in the design of a holistic rubric.

The need for headings as a means of clarification had begun to surface when working through the fourth step of the rubric construction process. When finishing the rubric in analytic form, it was becoming increasingly clear that headings might help to organize the emerging patterns. The initial rubric, in analytic form, may be found in table 6.1.

This spin-off on a grounded theory approach to essay analysis resulted in a large number of criteria. Using a long analytic rubric that scored each of these criteria as a separate entity would probably not have met the need for an equitable, formative, yet efficient system of scoring undergraduate essays.

The intended purpose of the rubric was to use it in a course where demonstration of the professional writing skills needed to produce a solid, quality product was important but not the content focus of the course. Rather than taking time to score the twenty-six strands in the analytic version of the rubric, the holistic rubric permits an overall score to be given based on *a majority or a preponderance of evidence*. With that purpose in mind, the analytic rubric was converted to a "pure form" holistic rubric, which may be found in table 6.2.

Once familiar with the components addressed in each strand, and if comfortable with the amount of criteria included in each of the cells under the three categories to be assessed, the rubric in table 6.2 could be a good fit for its intended purpose. However, if an initial reaction to table 6.2 is along the lines of "Too much! How can anyone be expected to decipher all of that?" especially for the large volume of text in the Writing Mechanics strand, the reader is not alone.

It was this author's reaction too. So what to do in order to avoid evaluating every single component individually, keep the overall leeway and flexibility of a holistic rubric, and build in some structure to augment the "at a glance" aspect of the rubric?

Try the same approach that may be used if coaching a piece of student writing where the information is good but needs organizational clarity: add headings. This can be done in several ways. Two will be provided here. The headings included in the first modified holistic rubric (see table 6.3) provide organizational clarity. They also provide a starting point for discussing some overriding areas of concrete, observable expectations for college-level writing with students.

What if the basic concept of a holistic rubric works but the rubric designer wants to provide a score that reflects individual criteria more accurately without reverting to an analytic rubric? The headings could be used as individual cells. The result is a modified version of a holistic rubric, as in table 6.4.

Table 6.1. Patterns of Errors in Written Narrative by Letter Grade: Analytic Rubric

Topic	A paper	B paper	C paper	D paper
Grammar				
Parallel Construction	Few or no errors	Minor errors	May be lacking or inaccurately used	Concerns about lack or inaccurate use
Pronoun-Noun Agreement	Minor pronoun-noun agreement errors	Some pronoun-noun agreement errors, esp. singular-plural	Many pronoun-noun agreement errors, esp. singular-plural	Many pronoun-noun agreement errors, esp. singular-plural
Sentence Structure	Usually grammatically correct, comfortable use of clauses and sentence structure	Overuse of two or more independent clauses in one sentence	Overuse of two or more independent clauses in one sentence; some sentences inverted, awkward use of clauses	Incomplete (lacking subject or predicate) and often very long sentences
Subject-Verb Agreement	Minor subject-verb agreement errors	Some subject-verb agreement errors	Many subject-verb agreement errors	Many subject-verb agreement errors
Writing Mechanics				
Accuracy of Information	Accurate	Accurate	Minor misinterpretation or inaccurate information	Perspectives inaccurate or based on misinterpreted information
Capitalization	Appropriate usage	Capitalizing too much when it is not needed	Capitalizing too much or minor inappropriate use of caps	Capitalizing too much or almost not at all or inconsistent/inappropriate use of caps
Clarity of Writing	Clear	Meaning of one or two sentences may be unclear	Meaning of a few sentences unclear	Meaning of some sentences unclear
Continuity	Transitions smooth	Transitions smooth, maybe one or two exceptions	Minor concerns about transitions from one paragraph to next	Concerns about transitions from one paragraph to next, moving from one topic to the next, and/or order of sentences within paragraphs
Generalizations	Generalizations avoided	Generalizations mostly avoided	Vague or sweeping ("All people would say . . .")	Vague or sweeping ("All people would say . . .")

(continued)

Table 6.1. (continued)

Topic	A paper	B paper	C paper	D paper
Missing Words	Missing one or two small words	Missing a word here or there	Missing a word here or there on almost every page	Missing a word here or there on almost every page
Paragraphs	One topic per paragraph	Minor concerns about too many topics in same paragraph	Some concerns about too many topics in same paragraph	Multipage paragraphs or no paragraphing; whole paper or section is one paragraph.
Perspective	Reasonable, appropriate perspectives	Appropriate perspectives	Exaggerations; overuse of *huge, major, most important*, etc.	Exaggerations or skewed, biased perspectives
Pictures	Not used	Not used	Cute graphics and pictures not appropriate for research paper	Cute graphics and pictures not appropriate for research paper may be used to make paper longer
Spelling	No errors	Usually no errors	Minor error or two	Spelling errors, including prefixes typed as separate words
Thesis Statement	Presented as a statement; addressed in summary	Presented as a question rather than a statement	May add a goal in the summary that was not addressed in the paper	May add a goal in the summary that was not addressed in the paper, and/or thesis not a strong focus of the paper
Thesis Statement Placement	Clearly stated in first paragraph or two	Included toward the end of the paper rather than clearly stated in first paragraphs	Included toward the end of the paper rather than clearly stated in first paragraphs	Included toward the end of the paper, or concerns about being able to identify a thesis statement
Writing Style	Consistent throughout	Usually consistent throughout	Sudden shift may cause reader to question originality	Mix of styles may cause reader to question originality

Punctuation				
Commas	Consistent placement of comma before *and* in sequence of three or more	Overuse of commas, before the *and* or *but* even if not a sequence of three or more	Too many commas, overused	Too many commas, overused, no apparent pattern of use
Punctuation and Direct Quotes	Incorrect placement of period when ending sentence with direct quote	Minor incorrect placement of punctuation pertaining to direct quotes	Some incorrect placement of punctuation pertaining to direct quotes	Incorrect/inconsistent placement of punctuation pertaining to direct quotes
APA Mechanics				
Anthropomorphism	Avoided	Usually avoided	Present ("This paper talks about . . .")	Present
Citing Titles in Text	No errors	No or few errors	Errors in underlining and capping book titles; placing quotation marks around journal titles	Errors in underlining and capping book titles; placing quotation marks around journal titles
Headings	Used accurately and effectively	Used effectively, usually accurately	Not used	Not used
In-Text Citations	Overciting; page number necessary only for direct quotes	Generally accurate use of all four citation methods	Some quoting of authors or sources (books) often missing year or page number	Extensive quoting of authors or sources (books) often missing year or extensive text blocks with much info but no supporting citations; no page number for direct quotes
Reference List	Predominately accurate APA	APA errors; may not even be double-spaced	APA errors; incorrect identification of author, esp. if corporate author	Does not look like an APA reference list and may be titled "Bibliography."
Reference List to Text Alignment	All references from text in reference list and vice versa	One or two references from text not in reference list or vice versa	A few references from text not in reference list or vice versa	Limited number of references; several references from text not in reference list or vice versa
References	No or minimal "n.d." references	Minimal "n.d." references	Many "n.d." references	Many "n.d." references or Wikipedia-type resources

Table 6.2. Patterns of Errors in Written Narrative by Letter Grade: Holistic Rubric

Topic	A paper	B paper	C paper	D paper
Grammar				
Parallel construction, Pronoun-noun agreement, Sentence structure, Subject-verb agreement	Few or no errors with parallel construction. Minor pronoun-noun errors. Usually grammatically correct, comfortable use of clauses and sentence structure. Minor subject-verb errors if any.	Minor errors with parallel construction. Some pronoun-noun agreement errors, esp. singular-plural. Overuse of two or more independent clauses in sentence. Subject-verb agreement errors.	Parallel construction lacking or inaccurately used in places. Many pronoun-noun errors, esp. singular-plural. Overuse of two or more independent clauses; some sentences inverted; awkward clause usage. Many subject-verb errors.	Concerns with lack of parallel construction or inaccurate use. Many pronoun-noun agreement errors, esp. singular-plural. Incomplete (lacking subject or predicate) and often very long sentences. Many subject-verb errors.
Writing Mechanics				
Accuracy of information, Capitalization, Clarity of writing, Continuity, Generalizations, Missing words, Paragraphs, Perspective, Pictures, Spelling, Thesis statement, Thesis statement placement, Writing style	Accurate information. Appropriate capitalization. Clear writing. Transitions smooth. Generalizations avoided. Missing one or two small words. One topic per paragraph. Reasonable, appropriate perspectives. Pictures not needed. No spelling errors. Thesis presented as a statement, addressed in	Accurate information. Capitalizing too much when it is not needed. Meaning of one or two sentences may be unclear. Transitions smooth, maybe one or two exceptions. Generalizations mostly avoided. Missing a word here or there. Minor concerns with too many topics in same paragraph. Appropriate perspectives. Pictures	Minor misinterpretation or inaccurate information. Capitalizing too much or minor inappropriate use of caps. Meaning of a few sentences unclear. Minor concerns about transitions from one paragraph to next. Vague and/or sweeping generalizations. Missing a word here or there on almost every page. Some concerns with too many topics in same paragraph.	Perspectives inaccurate or based on misinterpreted information. Capitalizing too much, almost not at all, or inconsistent/inappropriate use of capitalization. Meaning of some sentences unclear. Concerns about transitions from one paragraph to next, moving from one topic to the next, and/or order of sentences within paragraphs. Vague and/or sweeping

summary, clearly stated in first paragraph or two. Consistent writing style throughout.	not needed. Usually no spelling errors. Thesis presented as a question rather than a statement; included toward the end of the paper rather than clearly stated in first paragraphs. Usually consistent writing style throughout.	Exaggerations: overuse of *huge, major, most important,* etc. Cute graphics and pictures not appropriate for research paper. Minor spelling error or two. May add a goal in the summary that was not addressed in the paper. Thesis included toward the end of the paper rather than clearly stated in first paragraphs. Sudden shift in writing style may cause reader to question originality.	generalizations. Missing a word here or there on almost every page. Multipage paragraphs or no paragraphing: whole paper or section is one paragraph. Exaggerations or skewed, biased perspectives. Cute graphics and pictures not appropriate for research may be used to make paper longer. Spelling errors, including prefixes typed as separate words. May add a goal in the summary that was not addressed in the paper; and/or thesis not a strong focus of the paper, included toward the end of the paper, or concerns with being able to identify a thesis statement. Mix of writing styles may cause reader to question originality.

Punctuation
Commas,
Punctuation and direct quotes

Consistent placement of comma before and in sequence of three or more. Incorrect placement of period when ending sentence with direct quote.	Overuse of commas before *and* or *but* even if not a sequence of three or more. Minor incorrect placement of punctuation pertaining to direct quotes.	Too many commas, overused. Some incorrect placement of punctuation pertaining to direct quotes.	Too many commas, overused, no apparent pattern of use. Incorrect/ inconsistent placement of punctuation pertaining to direct quotes.

(continued)

Table 6.2. *(continued)*

Topic	A paper	B paper	C paper	D paper
APA Mechanics Anthropomorphism, Citing titles in text, Headings, In-text citations, Reference list, Reference list to text alignment, References	Anthropomorphism avoided. No text citation errors. Headings used effectively and accurately. Overciting: page numbers necessary only for direct quotes. Predominately accurate APA in reference list. All references from text in reference list and vice versa. No or minimal "n.d." references.	Anthropomorphism usually avoided. No or few text citation errors. Headings used effectively, usually accurately. Generally accurate use of all four citation methods. APA errors in reference list, may not even be double-spaced. One or two references from text not in reference list or vice versa. Minimal "n.d." references.	Anthropomorphism used ("This paper talks about . . ."). Errors in underlining and capping book titles; placing quotation marks around journal titles. Headings not used. Some quoting of authors or sources (books) often missing year and page number. APA errors in reference list; incorrect identification of author, esp. if corporate author. A few references from text not in reference list or vice versa. Many "n.d." references.	Anthropomorphism used ("This paper talks about . . ."). Errors in underlining and capping book titles; placing quotation marks around journal titles. Headings not used. Extensive quoting of authors or sources (books) often missing year or extensive text blocks with much info but no supporting citations, no page number for direct quotes. Does not look like an APA reference list and may be titled "Bibliography." Limited number of references; several references from text not in reference list or vice versa. Many "n.d." references or Wikipedia-type resources.

This particular holistic rubric is much closer to the analytic side of the design spectrum. Essentially, the difference between an analytic and a holistic rubric is more realistically considered not simply as dichotomous opposites. Analytic and holistic may be the anchor points on two ends of a continuum, but there are several points in between.

The rubric in table 6.4 would not work as an actual analytic rubric. Some of the individual components are described the same in two of the four columns. For example, the components of subject-verb agreement and headings are described the same in the C and D columns. Each strand contains specific criteria for each level, yet grouping multiple, similar categories of criteria in each strand allows for a choice of cell based on a majority or preponderance of the resulting evidence in each cell. This approach permits a score for the grouped criteria to be assigned by choosing the set of cell descriptors that most closely describes that aspect of the performance or product to be assessed without every aspect of the description in the cell needing to be its perfect fit.

Step 8. If a holistic rubric similar to the rubric in table 6.3 is used for scoring purposes with scores assigned by section, the instructor of record could adjust the weight of strands in one or more sections. This could be done so that the final score reflects the relative importance of the strands in contributing to the product or performance. In the example provided in table 6.3, the instructor may want to consider weighting the section of Writing Mechanics double simply because of the greater volume of criteria addressed in that section.

Step 9. In terms of piloting and then using this rubric, the actual recommendation was to provide the analytic version (see table 6.1) to students for purposes of checking their own work. The holistic rubric (any one of the three versions) would be used for scoring purposes. A rating system would need to be developed by the instructor to link the holistic rubric to the five-page essay assignment. Additional points could be earned for content or other course requirements addressed in the assignment and added to the number of points earned through the rubric to determine the total number of possible points for the assignment.

Step 10. When constructing rubrics for actual usage, the next steps would involve piloting and full implementation. The ten steps involved in the development of holistic rubrics may be found in the key considerations for this chapter.

The next chapter contains information regarding common errors in rubric design—some of which have already been touched upon in this chapter or previously in this book—that may interfere with implementation. If there have been less than optimal prior experiences with rubric assessment, a newly designed rubric is not working out as well as was hoped, or a rubric designer

Table 6.3. Patterns of Errors in Written Narrative Essays by Letter Grade Categories (Modified Holistic Rubric)

Writing Mechanics	A Papers	B Papers	C Papers	D Papers
Presentation of Information	Accurate information, appropriate perspectives, generalizations avoided.	Accurate information, appropriate perspectives, generalizations mostly avoided.	Minor misinterpreted or inaccurate information; some exaggerations, vagueness, or sweeping generalizations.	Concerns with misinterpreted, biased, or inaccurate info; exaggerations, vagueness, and/or sweeping generalizations.
Mechanical Elements	Correct capitals, punctuation, spelling; few or no missing words.	Capitals and/or commas overused, correct spelling, some missing words.	Capitals and/or commas overused or inappropriate, minor spelling errors, words missing on most pages.	Capitals and/or commas missing, overused, and/or incorrect with no patterns evident; spelling errors; words missing on every page.
Style	Writing and transitions easy to follow, single-topic paragraphs, appropriate graphics if any, consistent style throughout.	Writing and transitions mostly easy to follow, minor concerns with too many topics in same paragraph, appropriate graphics if any, usually consistent style.	Minor concerns about writing clarity and transitions, some concerns with too many topics in same paragraph, graphics or pictures not appropriate for thesis paper, sudden shifts in style may raise originality questions.	Concerns with writing clarity and transitions, too many topics in same paragraph or structure of paragraphs, graphics or pictures not appropriate for thesis paper or used to lengthen paper, sudden shifts in style may raise originality questions.
Thesis Statement	Thesis presented as a statement; addressed in summary, clearly stated in first paragraph or two. Consistent writing style throughout.	Thesis presented as a question and/or included toward the end of the paper rather than clearly stated in first paragraphs.	Thesis included toward the end of the paper rather than clearly stated in first paragraphs, may be info in summary that was not addressed in the paper.	Thesis not a strong focus of the paper, included toward end of paper, or cannot be identified; may be info in summary that was not addressed in the paper.

Grammar				
Sentence Structure	Few or no errors with parallel construction, use of clauses.	Minor errors with parallel construction, and overuse of independent clauses.	Errors with parallel construction, overuse of independent clauses and/or sentence structure may be awkward, inverted, or missing elements of a complete sentence.	Many errors with parallel construction; overuse of independent clauses and/or sentences may be very long and awkward; inverted or missing elements of a complete sentence.
Pronoun-Noun and Subject-Verb Agreement	Accurate noun-pronoun or subject-verb agreement.	Mostly accurate noun-pronoun or subject-verb agreement.	Some errors with noun-pronoun or subject-verb agreement.	Errors with noun-pronoun or subject-verb agreement, esp. singular-plural.
APA Mechanics				
Anthropomorphism	Avoided.	Usually avoided.	Present ("This paper talks about . . .").	Present.
APA Headings	Effective, accurate.	Effective, mostly accurate.	Ineffective or not used.	Not used.
In-Text Citation	Mostly accurate: may be overciting, page numbers where not needed, or incorrect punctuation of direct quotes.	No or few errors, may be incorrect punctuation of direct quotes.	Some errors in use of italics and punctuation, some in-text citations missing components.	Errors in use of italics and punctuation; in-text citations often missing components, or no sources cited.
Reference List	Mostly accurate APA, no "n.d." references, all references from text in reference list and vice versa.	May not be double-spaced, minimal "n.d." references, one or two references from text not in reference list or vice versa.	APA errors, incorrect ID of author, esp. if corporate; many "n.d." references; some references from text not in reference list or vice versa.	Does not look like APA reference list and may be titled "Bibliography," many "n.d." or Wikipedia-type resources, limited number references and/or several references from text not in reference list or vice versa.

Table 6.4. Patterns of Errors in Written Narrative Essays by Letter Grade Categories (Modified Holistic Rubric with Headings Used as Cell Strands)

Writing Mechanics	A Papers	B Papers	C Papers	D Papers
Presentation of Information	Accurate information, appropriate perspectives, generalizations avoided.	Accurate information, appropriate perspectives, generalizations mostly avoided.	Minor misinterpreted or inaccurate information; some exaggerations, vagueness, or sweeping generalizations.	Concerns with misinterpreted, biased, or inaccurate info; exaggerations, vagueness, and/or sweeping generalizations.
Mechanical Elements	Correct capitals, punctuation, spelling; few or no missing words.	Capitals and/or commas overused, correct spelling, some missing words.	Capitals and/or commas overused or inappropriate, minor spelling errors, words missing on most pages.	Capitals and/or commas missing, overused, and/or incorrect with no patterns evident; spelling errors; words missing on every page.
Style	Writing and transitions easy to follow, single-topic paragraphs, appropriate graphics if any, consistent style throughout.	Writing and transitions mostly easy to follow, minor concerns with too many topics in same paragraph, appropriate graphics if any, usually consistent style.	Minor concerns about writing clarity and transitions, some concerns with too many topics in same paragraph, graphics or pictures not appropriate for thesis paper, sudden shifts in style may raise originality questions.	Concerns with writing clarity and transitions, too many topics in same paragraph or structure of paragraphs, graphics or pictures not appropriate for thesis paper or used to lengthen paper, sudden shifts in style may raise originality questions.
Thesis Statement	Thesis presented as a statement; addressed in summary, clearly stated in first paragraph or two. Consistent writing style throughout.	Thesis presented as a question and/or included toward the end of the paper rather than clearly stated in first paragraphs.	Thesis included toward the end of the paper rather than clearly stated in first paragraphs, may be info in summary that was not addressed in the paper.	Thesis not a strong focus of the paper, included toward end of paper, or cannot be identified; may be info in summary that was not addressed in the paper.

Grammar				
Sentence Structure and Use of Clauses	Few or no errors with parallel construction, use of clauses.	Minor errors with parallel construction, and overuse of independent clauses.	Errors with parallel construction, overuse of independent clauses and/or sentence structure may be awkward, inverted, or missing elements of a complete sentence.	Many errors with parallel construction; overuse of independent clauses and/or sentences may be very long and awkward; inverted or missing elements of a complete sentence.
Noun-Pronoun and Subject-Verb Agreement	Accurate noun-pronoun or subject-verb agreement.	Mostly accurate noun-pronoun or subject-verb agreement.	Some errors with noun-pronoun or subject-verb agreement.	Errors with noun-pronoun or subject-verb agreement, esp. singular-plural.
APA Mechanics				
Anthropomorphism	Avoided.	Usually avoided.	Present ("This paper talks about . . .").	Present.
APA Headings	Effective, accurate.	Effective, mostly accurate.	Ineffective or not used.	Not used.
In-Text Citation	Mostly accurate: may be overciting, page numbers where not needed, or incorrect punctuation of quotes.	No or few errors, may be incorrect punctuation of direct quotes.	Some errors in use of italics and punctuation, some in-text citations missing components.	Errors in use of italics and punctuation; in-text citations often missing components, or no sources cited.
Reference List	Mostly accurate APA, no "n.d." references, all references from text in reference list and vice versa.	May not be double-spaced, minimal "n.d." references, one or two references from text not in reference list or vice versa.	APA errors, incorrect ID of author, esp. if corporate; many "n.d." references; some references from text not in reference list or vice versa.	Does not look like APA reference list and may be titled "Bibliography," many "n.d." or Wikipedia-type resources, limited number references and/or several references from text not in reference list or vice versa.

simply wants to head off potential complications when designing and implementing rubrics, chapter 7[AQ2] may provide some valuable assistance with problem solving.

KEY CONSIDERATIONS:
THE 10 STEPS IN HOLISTIC RUBRIC DEVELOPMENT

Step 1: Identify the goal of the assessment task and if it involves processes or products or both.

Step 2: Be sure a rubric is an effective, efficient assessment option.

Step 3: Determine if a holistic rubric is the best fit for your assessment task.

Step 4: Determine the criteria to be assessed in the rubric strands, listing as you encounter them, going back at a later time to arrange in alphabetical order (or other) and add headings if helpful for organization and clarity.

Step 5: Determine the column descriptors and the numerical scores, letter grades, or other rating systems.

Step 6: Determine the observable assessment criteria for each cell intersection of criterion and rating.

Step 7: If necessary, convert an analytic rubric developed to this point into a "pure form" holistic rubric by collapsing individual cells into larger cells and rewriting for clarity and grammatical flow. Group the criteria under headings if helpful.

Step 8: Consider whether or not to weight strands.

Step 9: Pilot and revise the rubric if necessary.

Step 10: Implement the rubric in practice.

7

A Closer Look at Rubric Strand Design

The basics of rubric design were addressed in chapters 5 (analytic rubrics) and 6 (holistic rubrics). Chapter 7 features a closer look at rubric strand design, a pivotal step in the construction of analytic or holistic rubrics. It also includes work with the design process and accompanying step-by-step rationale for a rubric the author developed several years ago.

The rubric was adopted by the United States Peace Corps for inclusion in their *Looking at Ourselves and Others* curriculum guide, a publication of World Wise Schools. Readers may recognize this as the program that connects returned Peace Corps volunteers with classroom teachers in grades three through twelve back in the United States. The rubric was developed to assess the impact of university-based service-learning projects on participants and members of a community.

This is the first step in the construction of any rubric: clearly identifying the goal of the assessment task at hand. That initial step includes clarifying whether the task involves assessing a longitudinal performance process or a dimension-contained product. Regardless of the approach selected, the most important consideration in rubric design is how well the resulting rubric strands assess what they are intended to assess. If posed as a question, how well do the components of the assessment instrument fit the assessment task?

As an aid in developing assessment rubrics that are a good fit for their respective assessment tasks, it may be helpful to ground the assessment tasks in some contextual information. One way to do this is to think like a traditional newspaper reporter in terms of the what, where, when, why, and who elements associated with the assessment task for which a rubric will be designed and used. Consider the following in any order that makes the most sense for thinking through a potential rubric:

What: The "what" addresses the course, degree program, clinical experience, field experience, project, selection process, or any other purpose for which you design a rubric. It also addresses any background the original designer may deem a good idea to provide for subsequent users of the rubric.

Where: This component is usually simple to identify, especially if the rubric is designed for use in a specific course, department, or unit on a specific campus. Keep notes with a list of questions that arise during the rubric development, piloting, and implementation processes in case you or someone else should need to revise the rubric at a later time.

When: This component is also a simple one and usually involves nothing more than a date; a semester, course, or section number; or a similar identification tag. Again, be specific and have a key readily available so that any related records are easy to locate and the coding is simple to decipher in another few months or in a few years. This could also refer to a point in the course or the program when the rubric is used.

Keep in mind that the intent of the rubric may be purely formative, used to assess work in progress, work completed at an entry level, or work-related projects completed over the course of a semester or program with higher levels of competence expected each time. On the other hand, the rubric may be intended for use only once, perhaps for a final project or clinical experience, as a summative assessment tool. A rubric may also fill both assessment needs, being used to assess work during the course of the class or program and again at the end as one final measure of summative skill. As is the case with any assessment instrument, using a rubric in an unintended manner or for an unintended purpose could interfere with or negate its effectiveness.

Why: This component provides a repository for notes addressing prior systems of project or process assessment and what the rubric was designed to accomplish. Notes would also involve the process of implementation and fine-tuning, and how the resulting data were used in a feedback loop to better equip program faculty to prepare professional candidates.

The latter is especially important should this information be needed for the endless record keeping common to professional program and institutional accreditation processes. It also provides a reminder to keep notes pertinent to evaluation procedures and ongoing efforts to provide developmental assessment, usually course based, to students.

Although rubrics are most often designed for the assessment of student work, they are not limited to that purpose. They can be used to teach processes of reasoning or serve as a self-assessment guide to prevent students from making inadvertent errors. Rubrics can also be used to show students where gaps exist in their understanding or mastery of a defined bank of knowledge, or to compare and contrast the relative merits of two or more courses of action.

Who: Describe the students or other persons the rubric will be used to assess or guide. What pertinent knowledge is expected when they enter the course or experience in which the rubric will be implemented? Are there course prerequisites? Is the rubric designed for a specific clinical rotation or year of an internship?

With some context in place, the goal of the rubric to be constructed is easier to identify and the project or process will already have been clarified. The strand descriptors will be easier to identify and the strands can subsequently be more readily developed. For our purposes here, let us accept the premise that a rubric will be a good fit for the assessment task the reader has at hand and that you have reached the step in which cell language needs to be drafted.

Seven basic approaches tend to be used for drafting descriptor language and assembling the individual strands: simple additive, sequential additive, developmental, descriptive, quality enhanced, quantity structured, and alignment based. A description of each follows, with rubric strand examples. The purpose of presenting these is not to make the reader adept at distinguishing an additive rubric strand from an incremental. As long as the strand and cell language fits the assessment task, it really makes no difference. However, a look at some different approaches to writing rubric strand descriptor language can (1) help rubric designers find an easy way to get started by crafting a few examples of each, (2) provide a list of alternate approaches to take if a designer or design team experiences writer's block when writing descriptor language, and (3) provide alternatives to consider if a rubric is not doing what was hoped it would and its designers are not sure why.

SIMPLE ADDITIVE STRAND DESIGN

Additive strands assess an overall skill by specifying the ever-increasing aspects of a given skill that need to be observed to indicate that a student's skill level is increasing. When beginning to construct simple additive rubric strands, instead of drafting the outside extremes and working in from there, it may be more helpful to begin on the side of the rubric describing the highest level of competence to be addressed. List all of the aspects of the skill that need to be attained to achieve that level for purposes of the assessment being developed. For example, if the overall skill to be demonstrated is writing with correct APA style, a rubric strand for that skill at the initial phase of design could look like the strand in table 7.1.

Table 7.1. Simple Additive Rubric Strand: Demonstrating APA Style Competency

	Initial Skill	*Developing*	*Competent*	*Highly Competent*
APA Style Competence				Accurate APA cover page, grammar, punctuation, in-text references, and reference list

With that in place, decrease the number of aspects in which skill needs to be demonstrated as you work back across the rubric. Be sure that the number of aspects indicated for "Competent," or an equivalent level descriptor, is what you would need to see as a basic passing level of skill attainment. An example of a completed additive rubric strand appears in table 7.2.

There is a basic assumption at work with all additive rubrics. Skills essential to the overall skill that have already been demonstrated are maintained as one moves across the rubric. As the rubric strand is developed from the lowest to the highest point value, additional skills are added, in batches or individually. The latter is the case in this rubric example. In all additive rubrics, the emphasis is on the accumulation of skill components relative to one overriding skill and not on the process involved in developing one or more of those individual skill components.

In a simple additive rubric, the number of skill aspects demonstrated increases as the number of points to be earned in the strand increases. However, the aspects of the overall skill to be attained do not need to be accumulated in a specific sequence or order. An additive rubric helps an instructor assess how much of an overall skill can be demonstrated. Descriptor language in the cells within additive strands answers the question, "How many components of the overall skill have been mastered?" This differs somewhat from sequential additive rubrics.

Table 7.2. Simple Additive Rubric Strand: Demonstrating APA Style Competency

	Initial Skill	*Developing*	*Competent*	*Highly Competent*
APA Style Competence	Fewer than three of the target competencies	Three of the five target competencies	All but one of the target competencies	Accurate APA cover page, grammar, punctuation, in-text references, and reference list

Table 7.3. Sequential Additive Rubric Strand: Making Dinner

	Initial Skill	Developing	Competent	Highly Competent
Making Dinner	Can make dessert			

SEQUENTIAL ADDITIVE STRAND DESIGN

When designing a sequential additive rubric strand, it may be helpful to begin on the opposite side of the strand, with the lowest level of competence to be addressed. To consider a noneducational example, if someone is learning to make dinner, they will probably start by learning to make one course. Dessert is a common starting point. On a rubric, this looks as indicated in table 7.3.

When working with a sequential additive rubric, components of the overall skill would be added as the rubric designer progresses across the rubric strand. Three assumptions are in play here. The first is the same as for simple additive rubrics. Skill components essential to the overall skill that have already been demonstrated are maintained as one moves across the rubric and additional skills are added.

The second assumption is that basic skill competence needs to be in place for each skill component before it can be recognized as attained. For example, suppose that a student of making dinner was producing brownies that could be poured out of the pan after baking as well as before. Clearly the initial skill level—defined as "Can make dessert"—has not yet been attained. Once the brownies can be baked, cut, and served as a dessert, the culinary student could be said to have attained the basic skill needed to make a dessert. This would place the student's skill level in the "Initial Skill" column of the rubric in table 7.4. When the student has also mastered the skill of making a salad, the student's skill level would be defined as "Developing" in the completed rubric strand.

Table 7.4. Sequential Additive Rubric Strand: Making Dinner

	Initial Skill	Developing	Competent	Highly Competent
Making Dinner	Can make dessert	Can make dessert and a salad	Can make dessert, a salad, and a main course	Can make dessert, a salad, a main course, and fresh bread

The third assumption, pertinent only to sequential additive rubrics, is that the components need to be added in a predetermined order. For example, what if the culinary student can make a palatable dessert, salad, and bread, but main courses are still being refused even by four-legged canine members of the family? The cooking student would remain at the developing level.

If skills are attained out of the specified order, or sequence, in a sequential additive rubric, the competency rating is still determined by the lowest level in which all aspects are demonstrated. If aspects from higher rubric levels are already in place, that may result in the missing step being put in place soon. However, until that takes place, the strand level of the missing step has not yet been attained. Once it is demonstrated, the next level of the rubric has been reached.

To summarize, those are the two main differences between simple additive rubrics and sequential additive rubrics. In a sequential additive rubric, the aspects of the overall skill to be attained need to be accumulated in a specific sequence or order. Basic skill competence also needs to be in place for each sequentially added component before it can be considered attained and the student is ready to work toward the next level on the rubric.

A sequential additive rubric helps an instructor assess how many aspects of an overall skill have been accumulated in a specific order or sequence. Descriptor language in the cells within sequential additive strands answers the question, "How many sequential steps toward the overall skill have been taken?"

DEVELOPMENTAL STRAND DESIGN

Working from the minimal skill level in the rubric to the outer levels is help-ful with developmental cell design. The basic premise is similar to additive strand design, but developmental cells differ from additive cells in one key area. Skills are expanded as one moves across the strand rather than accumu-lating several different skills or aspects of an overall skill. Rubrics are inher-ently developmental in nature, and developmental strands are one of the most common forms of rubric strand design.

As a simple nonacademic example, if a rubric were designed to assess a baby's developmental progress in learning to walk, the minimal skill level de-scriptor for the strand "Learning to Walk" would be something along the lines of "Can take one or two steps unassisted." If that were used as the cell descrip-tion, the initial work on the strand would look like the example in table 7.5.

The rubric designer would use this inner cell minimum competence level as a starting point and work from there to define descriptor values for the re-

Table 7.5. Developmental Rubric Strand: Learning to Walk

	Undeveloped Skill Level	*Developing Skill Level*	*Minimal Skill Level*	*Advancing Skill Level*	*Advanced Skill Level*
Learning to Walk Unassisted			Can take one or two steps unassisted		

Table 7.6. Developmental Rubric Strand: Learning to Walk

	Undeveloped Skill Level	*Developing Skill Level*	*Minimal Skill Level*	*Advancing Skill Level*	*Advanced Skill Level*
Learning to Walk Unassisted	Cannot yet stand and maintain a standing position		Can take one or two steps unassisted		Can walk throughout the house and is beginning to run

mainder of the cells. At this point, it is helpful to define the outer skill levels, usually variants of "undeveloped" and "advanced," as in table 7.6.

With the minimal skill level defined and the outer levels described, the transitional levels on either side of the minimal skill can be defined as in table 7.7.

The basic design approach for a developmental rubric or rubric strand stems from a perspective of developmental growth over time, as in the above example, or as the result of increasing proficiency. Descriptor language in the

Table 7.7. Developmental Rubric Strand: Learning to Walk

	Undeveloped Skill Level	*Developing Skill Level*	*Minimal Skill Level*	*Advancing Skill Level*	*Advanced Skill Level*
Learning to Walk Unassisted	Cannot yet reach and maintain a standing position	Can pull self up and stand, with or without assistance; may take steps holding on to an object or person	Can take one or two steps unassisted	Can take several steps unassisted	Can walk throughout the house and is beginning to run

cells within incremental strands answers the question, "How strong has the demonstration of this component become?"

DESCRIPTIVE STRAND DESIGN

When crafting a descriptive strand, the rubric designer could work from one side to the other or use the technique of defining the outer levels first and working in from there. An assessment rubric, by its nature, is designed so that what is described in the cells in higher-scoring columns is valued more than what is described in the lower scoring columns. Despite this aspect of inherent value infusion, it is possible and sometimes desirable to craft rubric strands that are not value based. In the example in table 7.8, none of the cell descriptions are better than the others. All assume a basic level of quality in the product (in this case) described in each cell. Some are valued more than others by no system of merit other than the rubric designer's choice.

When done well, descriptive strands are the essence of rubric assessment because they simply, objectively describe desired behaviors or conditions of performance or accomplishment, free of value-imbedded terminology. In a pure-form descriptive rubric, all of the cells describe performance or product attributes that aren't inherently better in and of themselves. For example, suppose an instructor wanted students to design a simple PowerPoint presentation for a course assignment but not devote time to adding the "bells and whistles" of clip art, animation, or links. The rubric strand for that component could just as easily look like the strand in table 7.9.

There is nothing inherently right or wrong about the descriptions in each of the cells used in tables 7.8 and 7.9. The hierarchical levels are determined solely by what is needed or desired for this particular performance or product.

If you have musical background, or eclectic music tastes, try thinking of the difference in terms of performance style. There is nothing inherently right or wrong about singing in a sultry jazz style or with the vocal athleticism required to smoothly execute lengthy melismatic passages in a Handel aria.

Table 7.8. Descriptive Rubric Strand: PowerPoint Slides for a Presentation I

Level	1	2	3
Component			
PowerPoint Slides	PowerPoint slides with colored background and speaker's notes	PowerPoint slides with pictures, clip art, or charts	PowerPoint slides with animation, movies, or sound

Table 7.9. Descriptive Rubric Strand: PowerPoint Slides for a Presentation II

Level	1	2	3
Component			
PowerPoint Slides	PowerPoint slides with animation, movies, or sound	PowerPoint slides with pictures, clip art, or charts	PowerPoint slides with colored background and speaker's notes

However, jazz mechanics would rank in the lowest rubric level if describing the vocal style to be demonstrated in a late Baroque aria—and Baroque-era opera or oratorio performance practices are not a good fit for singing classic jazz. Descriptor language in the cells within descriptive rubric strands provides an answer to the question, "How well does the performance or finished product fit requirements of this component within this context?"

QUALITY-ENHANCED STRAND DESIGN

The quality-enhanced rubric strand design is very different in that it relies on value to assist assessors in delineating levels of good, better, and best in terms of performance or product. Consider the example of assessing a young child going through kindergarten entry tests in gross motor skills. The ability to walk is good, to jump on two feet better, to hop on one foot better yet, and to skip is the best and most highly rated of all those options. The task of

Table 7.10. Quality-Enhanced Rubric Strand: Context-Based Description of Student

Level	3	2	1	0
Description of Student to Be Evaluated and Context	Specific data-focused description of student to be evaluated (demographics, strengths/weaknesses in content area) and student's class (demographics, size, range of abilities)	Clear descriptions of student to be studied (demographics, strengths/weaknesses in content area) and student's class (demographics, size, range of abilities)	Minimal or nonspecific descriptions of student (demographics, strengths/weaknesses in content area) and student's class (demographics, size, range of abilities)	Missing descriptions of student and/or student's class, or the information provided leaves unanswered questions regarding student or class context

designing this kind of strand can be approached from the outside in or across the row, whichever is easier for the rubric designer and whichever works best with the content of the strand.

In the sample holistic rubric strand in table 7.10, educational psychology students are being assessed on their ability to describe a child being evaluated in an elementary school classroom context.

Descriptor language in the cells within quality-enhanced rubric strands differs from a developmental rubric in that descriptive ratings are based on the student's level of accomplishment in demonstrating the particular skill or producing the desired product. Quality-enhanced rubric strand language answers the question, "How well is this component produced or enacted?"

QUANTITY-STRUCTURED STRAND DESIGN

Strands featuring quantity structure are easy to spot because they usually contain numerical descriptions. They are also easy to fall back on, perhaps too easy at times, because it is often much simpler to say, "It needs more," than to linger over the wordsmithing involved in determining more of *what* and how that looks. While that trap is to be avoided, quantitative descriptions are often the best means of describing levels of performance.

This is the case whether one is assessing the number of revolutions in an ice-skating or dance routine, weight-bearing capability of a newly designed structure, or the number of credible resources in a graduate research paper. In some cases, the more representations of a given descriptor, the better the

Table 7.11.   Quantity-Structured Rubric Strand: Professional Philosophy Statement

Level	0	1	2	3	4
Well Referenced	Fewer than three references	Three references, one of which may be drawn from classical or modern literature	Four references, one of which may be drawn from classical or modern literature	Five references, one of which may be drawn from classical or modern literature	Five or more references, plus one or more references from classical or modern literature
Edited Copy upon Submission	>7 typo, APA, or mechanical errors	6–7 typo, APA, or mechanical errors	4–5 typo, APA, or mechanical errors	2–3 typo, APA, or mechanical errors	0–1 typo, APA, or mechanical errors

rubric score. At other times, less is more, as when assessing the number of mechanical errors in a finished product. Examples of strands in which high or low numbers are preferred may be found in the example in table 7.11.

Returning again to the example of a child, a capability to fluently read fifty words per minute is better than fluently reading twenty or thirty words a minute. Descriptor language in the cells within quantity-structured rubric strands answers the question, "How closely does the number of components in this cell align with the desired number for this strand?"

ALIGNMENT-BASED STRAND DESIGN

The final strand type, that of alignment-based design, is primarily germane to research papers, technical reports, and written work of this nature. This kind of rubric strand can assist in the consideration of the strength of references in text. It can also refer to fit of a performance or product with accepted standards of practice, safety guidelines, research basis of a decision or choice, or adherence to rules or policies, as in the example provided in table 7.12.

Table 7.12. Standards-Aligned Rubric Strand: Safety Inspection Report

Level	0	1	2	3
State and National Standard Alignment	Report not fully aligned with state or national standards	Report fully aligned with state or national standards	Report aligned with most state and national standards	Report fully aligned with state and national standards

Rubrics or rubric strands of this type are common when assessing the infusion of professional standards in action, work samples, or academic programs. Descriptor language in the cells within alignment-based rubric strands is designed to provide an answer to the question, "How well does this component conform to established standards?"

STRAND DESIGNS IN APPLICATION:
THE PEACE CORPS SERVICE-LEARNING RUBRIC

An analytic rubric that offers an example of several kinds of rubric strand design is provided here. The traditional reporters' questions are used to provide contextual background prior to highlighting five of the seven kinds of strand design.

What: The Peace Corps rubric had its genesis as part of a Learn and Serve America grant-funded initiative. One component of the grant involved disbursement of funds to pairs of student teachers and their supervising cooperating teachers who voluntarily engaged in professional development to learn how to enact service-learning projects in their classrooms.

Where: The service-learning project was based in Iowa City and involved all three regents' universities in Iowa. The author was an assistant professor at the University of Northern Iowa at the time and served as UNI's site coordinator for the grant.

When: The grant in question spanned a three-year period from 1994 to 1997 that involved six fall or spring semesters. The rubric was initially implemented during this time. It was subsequently adopted by the United States Peace Corps to use as a guide when developing and assessing national or international service-learning projects.

Why: The service-learning rubric was needed because K–12 teachers, student teachers, and administrators—essentially, everyone involved in the project with the exception of the three site coordinators—were completely or relatively new to the concept of service learning. They were familiar with service and, of course, with learning, but the unique hybrid created by a blending of the two was not yet familiar.

To their credit, they were willing to attempt something not yet seen much in practice at the time, when service learning was just beginning to make an appearance in P–16 settings. In the absence of myriad local examples, a rubric was desired not so much to assess finished service-learning projects but to guide and help shape the direction of works in progress.

Who: This service-learning rubric was initially used for students in their final semesters of teacher-preparation programs. Students in a variety of specific content area and grade-level disciplines were involved, mostly traditional undergraduates but some MAT or semi-lateral entry students. Practicing classroom teachers were paired with each student; experience levels ranged from almost three years to more than thirty years.

With some context in place, the goal was easier to identify and the project or process to be assessed was clarified. In the case of the service-learning rubric, the goal was to provide an instrument that would help teachers make conscious decisions regarding how close the service-learning projects to be designed would come to the theoretical ideals of service learning. The theoretical ideals and desired outcomes of service learning were expressed in seven areas to be considered when implementing a service-learning project with K–12 students.

These seven areas became the seven components that formed the basis for the rubric strands down the left side of the rubric. This rubric was designed to describe how these seven components would look in classroom-related practice at varying levels of service-learning impact that ranged from strong to minimal. The rubric needed to be applicable to many different kinds of circumstances or assessment tasks and the resulting processes.

Yes, tangible products would be produced. But the processes of serving were the focal points; the outcomes were, for the most part, intangible. Therefore, this was an example of a rubric designed to assess process rather than product.

The first rubric strand is an example of alignment-based design. It was created to help participants consider the level at which the service-learning project meets actual community needs. The cells in the strand describe the levels at which this is determined through current research as opposed to old research, guessing at community needs, or not addressing this key component at all, which would violate the authenticity of the service-learning project.

The second strand, in which the collaboration component was covered, is an example of developmental strand design. The involvement of community members grew from the level of no or coincidental knowledge to levels describing active, direct collaboration.

The third strand is a good example of a descriptive strand because each of the cells in and of itself contains an acceptable classroom practice. Whether as an instructional strategy, teaching technique, curricular component, or curricular supplement, service learning can be a valuable addition to the classroom. For purposes of this grant however, the ideal was to integrate service learning as an instructional strategy, thus this description's position in the highest-level cell of the strand.

The fourth is an example of a quality-enhanced strand. It started from a basis of students providing a summary of events and expanded to the point of their sharing with each other. It then progressed to collaborating on group reflection and finally moved on to individual and group reflections.

The fifth strand, though it does not contain numbers, is quantity structured. The main difference between the cells focused on the involvement of no, some, most, or all students in experiencing application of the new academic skill or knowledge in a real-world setting.

The sixth and seventh strands are examples of quality-enhanced components. The sixth addressed student reflections that move from self-centered pros and cons to affective reflection perspectives. The seventh addressed the impact of changes upon quality of life resulting from the service-learning project. The full service-learning rubric may be viewed in table 7.13.

To summarize, most of the strands constructed for analytic rubrics can be categorized as meeting or coming close to one of seven strand designs: additive, sequential additive, developmental, descriptive, quality enhanced, quan-

Table 7.13. The Service-Learning Rubric

	Strong Impact	Good Impact	Some Impact	Minimal Impact
1. Meet actual community need (*Alignment based*)	Determined by current research conducted or discovered by students with teacher assistance where appropriate	Determined by past research discovered by students with teacher assistance where appropriate	Determined by making a guess at what community needs may be	Community needs secondary to a project teacher wants to do; project considers only student needs
2. Are coordinated in collaboration with community (*Developmental*)	Active, direct collaboration with community by the teacher and/or student	Community members act as consultants in the project development	Community members are informed of the project directly	Community members are coincidentally informed or not knowledgeable at all
3. Are integrated into academic curriculum (*Descriptive*)	Service learning as instructional strategy with content/service components integrated	Service learning as a teaching technique with content/service components concurrent	Service learning part of curriculum but sketchy connections, with emphasis on service	Service learning supplemental to curriculum, in essence just a service project or good deed
4. Facilitate active student reflection (*Quality enhanced*)	Students think, share, produce reflective products individually and as group members	Students think, share, produce group reflection only	Students share with no individual reflective projects	Ran out of time for true reflection; just provided a summary of events

5. Use new academic skill/ knowledge in real-world settings (*Quantity structured*)	All students have direct application of new skill or knowledge in community service	Most students have some active application of new skill or knowledge	Some students more involved than others or little community-service involvement	Skill knowledge used mostly in the classroom; no active community-service experience
6. Help develop sense of caring for and about others (*Quality enhanced*)	Reflections show affective growth regarding self in community and the importance of service	Reflections show generic growth regarding the importance of community service	Reflections restricted to pros and cons of particular service project regarding the community	Reflections limited to self-centered pros and cons of the service project
7. Improve quality of life for person(s) served (*Quality enhanced*)	Facilitate change or insight; help alleviate a suffering; solve a problem; meet a need or address an issue	Changes enhance an already good community situation	Changes mainly decorative, but new and unique benefits realized in community	Changes mainly decorative, of limited community benefit, or are not new and unique

tity structured, or alignment based. The strand designs and the accompanying questions answered by the cells in each type of strand may be found in the key considerations for chapter 7.

KEY CONSIDERATIONS: QUESTIONS ANSWERED BY THE SEVEN TYPES OF RUBRIC STRANDS

Simple Additive—How many components of the overall skill have been mastered?

Additive Sequential—How many sequential steps toward the overall skill have been taken?

Developmental—How strong has the demonstration of this component become?

Descriptive—How well does the performance or finished product fit requirements of this component within this context?

Quality Enhanced—How well is this component produced or enacted?

Quantity Structured—How closely does the number of components in this cell align with the desired number for this strand?

Alignment Based—How well does this component conform to established standards?

REFERENCE

United States Peace Corp (n.d.). Looking at ourselves and others. Retrieved from http://wws.peacecorps.gov/wws/publications/looking/pdf/LookingatOurselvesand Others.pdf.

8

Common Errors in Rubric Design

A rubric is only as good as the quality of its design and the manner in which it is used, as is the case with any assessment tool. Helping rubric designers and users avoid common errors in order to ensure quality in rubric design and a smoother, more effective implementation is the underlying intent of this chapter. Rubrics need to be specific, include every component essential to the desired performance or product, and be easily understood by the assessor, the person or persons to be assessed, and anyone else who views or uses data associated with the rubric assessment process.

When instructors express a lack of interest in rubric assessment, it is inevitably because they have not worked firsthand with rubrics, have an incomplete understanding of rubric implementation, or have encountered problems with using rubrics stemming from flaws in essential elements of their design. This chapter by no means addresses all potential errors, but it does focus on common design errors involving descriptors, inclusion of key components, weighting, numerical values, criteria consistency, and format.

COMMON ERROR #1:
USING VAGUE, NONSPECIFIC DESCRIPTORS

Problems with descriptors can arise when determining the observable assessment criteria in each of the cells within the body of the rubric. Values-based descriptors such as "poor," "limited," "good," "above average," or "exemplary" may work as descriptors for column headings. As cell descriptors, especially stand-alone cell descriptors, they leave rubric ratings open to a degree of subjective interpretation that compromises rubric effectiveness.

Remember that the overall purpose of a rubric is to make the process of assessment, which tends to be inherently subjective, more objective, more behavior specific, and more criterion based. The task in designing assessment criteria descriptors involves determining a degree of specificity that provides the instructor the means to evaluate with language that fits the assessment task. This is done to preserve the highest possible degree of fairness and equity in the assessment process.

For example, consider the rubric strand in table 8.1, which assesses the degree to which a paper or project is aligned with a set of hypothetical professional standards. The goal for students is to directly align their work with at least one standard. If students do this, they attain a level-three rating on the rubric. To align work with more than one standard would exceed expectations, rating a four on the rubric.

The example does not provide the information of whether or not a given student aligned his or her work with one or with more than one standard. It also does not provide a student with the expectation of direct alignment. Furthermore, students and instructors may have difficulty distinguishing between a paper that is "poorly" aligned with standards and one that is "somewhat," or between a paper or project that is simply aligned with standards as opposed to "very" aligned with standards.

The example does provide the opportunity for instructors to credit students for attempting standards alignment. Students doing so can earn a two on the rubric even if they have not achieved the desired level of alignment that would have earned a three. Essentially, the rubric strand in table 8.1 provides a Likert scale in a matrix and suffers from the same problems concerning subjectivity and lack of specific performance criteria that usually categorize Likert scale assessments.

Contrast the rubric strand in table 8.1 with the strand in table 8.2. The goal remains the same. Students need to directly align their work with at least one professional standard. The observable assessment criterion for a rating of zero remains the same: the paper or project is not aligned with standards. But instead of a vague value descriptor of "poorly," the rubric defines "poor" as indirect alignment by using language that is specific to the task. In the

Table 8.1.   Alignment with Professional Standards (4 Possible Points)

Criteria	0	1	2	3	4
Aligned with Professional Standards	Not aligned with standards	Poorly aligned with standards	Somewhat aligned with standards	Aligned with standards	Very aligned with standards

Table 8.2. Alignment with Professional Standards (4 Possible Points)

Criteria	0	1	2	3	4
Aligned with Professional Standards	Not aligned with standards	Indirectly aligned	Aligned with at least one standard	Directly aligned with at least one standard	Directly aligned with at least two standards

example in table 8.2, a clear distinction is made between levels one and two. This retains the opportunity for instructors to credit students for attempting standards alignment even if the resulting quality is not yet at the level of a three on the rubric. It also gives a student a much clearer picture of what needs to be done to attain a higher-level rating.

An instructor using this rubric strand would be wise to provide prior examples of what constitutes "indirect" and "direct" alignment, and provide exercises designed to help students convert "aligned" work to "directly aligned" work. If this preparation were not provided, the "directly aligned" descriptor could be considered vague and the "indirect" descriptor may be confusing.

Moving to the upper end of the rubric, the top rubric descriptor specifies that the work to be assessed must be clearly aligned with at least two standards to earn the rating of a four. If a student would attempt alignment with more than one standard but do so in a vague, incomplete, unclear manner, the resulting work could still be rated a two on the rubric. This is the case because that level specifies alignment with "at least one" standard. All possibilities are covered, using descriptor language specific to the work that is to be assessed.

COMMON ERROR #2: MISSING KEY COMPONENTS

The second common error involves the fourth step of rubric design: determining the criteria to be assessed. If a criterion is omitted or if criteria are included that are nonessential to the performance or product to be assessed, the resulting composite score will not provide a meaningful comprehensive evaluation of student work.

For example, for a hypothetical written project, students were required to provide a standards-aligned fifteen-minute PowerPoint presentation that profiled the historical background associated with an American political party of the student's choice with flawless mechanical copy. The first assessment strand would determine if the work is directly aligned with standards, borrowing the same criteria descriptors from table 8.2. The second strand would address the quality of the PowerPoint treatment provided. The third would address topical content. The fourth strand would address mechanical elements of the edited copy, with the hope of finding no typographical, grammatical, or style (APA, MLA) errors.

The composite objective in this case is to provide a well-prepared PowerPoint presentation with accurate, concise, standards-aligned content and flawless writing mechanics. If the first strand was omitted from the rubric and the presentation was of good quality with accurate, concise information and no mechanical errors, it would be possible to attain a high composite rubric score even if there was no mention of standards alignment.

If the second strand was omitted, the flow of the PowerPoint presentation could be disjointed or the student could decide to submit the project on paper instead of in PowerPoint format. There would be no means of reflecting this in the composite rubric grade.

If the third strand was omitted, the topical treatment could be superficial, inaccurate, off topic, not referenced, or too text laden for clarity. The result would still be a high rubric score.

And if the final strand was omitted, it would be possible to have excellent work marred by the distraction of mechanical errors—and a composite rubric score that did not indicate this concern. This would not provide students with the specific feedback they would need to do a better job on subsequent projects. If any of these four strands were omitted, the resulting rubric score would not provide an accurate description of the composite work required to complete a high-quality project as defined by these four components.

In like manner, if a nonessential component were included in the rubric strands, the resulting composite would also provide an inaccurate, or at best unrealistic, assessment result. A rubric that assesses the cover design of a hard-copy portfolio or the hue and test weight of the paper used would result in students earning or losing points that have little or nothing to do with key components of the performance task.

These kinds of criteria may be specified as requirements for a given product, but they belong in a contextual introduction. If deemed absolutely necessary, peripheral components can be collapsed into one rubric strand as presentation requirements rather than presented as discrete items on a rubric that assesses key elements.

Instead, all four strands that make up essential elements of this particular project are addressed in the rubric in table 8.3, using descriptor language specific to the task to be assessed. It is clear what needs to be done to "go the extra mile" and earn a four on the rubric in each strand. Every possible combination of product quality on these four key elements is reflected in the rubric strands. The resulting rubric scores will provide accurate numerical pictures of the products students have produced.

Table 8.3. Prepare a Fifteen-Minute, Standards-Aligned PowerPoint Presentation Addressing the Historical Background of an American Political Party (16 Possible Points)

Criteria	0	1	2	3	4
Aligned with Professional Standards	Not aligned with standards	Indirectly aligned	Aligned with at least one standard	Directly aligned with at least one standard	Directly aligned with at least two standards
Fifteen-Minute PowerPoint Preparation	Not in PowerPoint format or exceeds the time limit	Ineffective design or sequencing of presentation	Effort to design and sequence the presentation is apparent	Effectively designed and sequenced presentation	Effectively designed and sequenced presentation, tech enhanced
Historical Background	Multiple inaccuracies or no use of secondary sources	Vague information or minor inaccuracies; used secondary sources	Accurate information; used five or fewer secondary sources	Accurate information; used more than five secondary sources	Accurate information; used more than five secondary sources and at least one primary source
Edited Copy	>7 typo, APA, or mechanical errors	6–7 typo, APA, or mechanical errors	4–5 typo, APA, or mechanical errors	2–3 typo, APA, or mechanical errors	0–1 typo, APA, or mechanical error

COMMON ERROR #3:
OMITTING CONSIDERATION OF WEIGHTED ELEMENTS

On the opposite end of avoiding too much emphasis on criteria that are not key components of a product or performance task comes the issue of dealing with criteria that are especially essential to the task being assessed. There may be one or more strands that are extremely essential to the performance or product, to the point that the overall composite score would yield an inaccurate picture of overall quality if the element were not emphasized. It is also possible that an instructor may simply want to emphasize one or more of the components over others for instructional purposes. In such cases it is possible to weight one or more strands by counting the rubric points earned in the strand more than once when determining the composite rubric score.

Consider the assessment task in table 8.4, to evaluate the PowerPoint presentation on the historical background of an American political party. While all the strands were key elements, the most important could easily be perceived to be the content information to be gathered and presented to meet the requirements described in the third strand. In this case, the third strand could be doubly weighted, counted twice when determining the composite rubric score.

The total number of points it is possible to earn on this rubric would now be 20, as indicated in table 8.4. So a student who had earned a four on each strand of the rubric would receive a composite rubric score of 20 rather than 16 (4 + 4 + [4 + 4] + 4 = 20), because the score of four for the third rubric strand would be counted twice.

COMMON ERROR #4: ASSIGNING
A RANGE OF NUMERICAL VALUES TO A COLUMN

As mentioned in a previous chapter, this is perhaps the most frequently observed error and the easiest one to correct. Providing a range of numerical scores is usually intended to make a rubric more flexible and better able to accurately reflect the overall quality of the performance or product.

I fully expect some readers to disagree with me on this point and retain the practice of using a range of scores in rubric columns because it has become so prevalent. If this is done, do it by choice and with full awareness of potential implementation problems or accusations of bias. Providing a range of score values for a rubric column makes it impossible to fairly and accurately provide equitable composite rubric scores for all members of a class or to equitably convert those rubric scores to letter grades. This may be one of the

Table 8.4. Prepare a Fifteen-Minute, Standards-Aligned PowerPoint Presentation Addressing the Historical Background of an American Political Party (20 Possible Points)

Criteria	0	1	2	3	4
Aligned with Professional Standards	Not aligned with standards	Indirectly aligned	Aligned with at least one standard	Directly aligned with at least one standard	Directly aligned with at least two standards
Fifteen-Minute PowerPoint Preparation	Not in PowerPoint format or exceeds the time limit	Ineffective design or sequencing of presentation	Effort to design and sequence the presentation is apparent	Effectively designed and sequenced presentation	Effectively designed and sequenced presentation, tech enhanced
Historical Background (Weight: x2)	Multiple inaccuracies or no use of secondary sources	Vague information or minor inaccuracies; used secondary sources	Accurate information; used five or fewer secondary sources	Accurate information; used more than five secondary sources	Accurate information; used more than five secondary sources and at least one primary source
Edited Copy	>7 typo, APA, or mechanical errors	6–7 typo, APA, or mechanical errors	4–5 typo, APA, or mechanical errors	2–3 typo, APA, or mechanical errors	0–1 typo, APA, or mechanical error

reasons why some academic course management programs do not provide an option to enter more than one numerical score per rubric column.

For example, in the four-strand rubric in table 8.5, columns have been assigned a two-digit range of numerical values. If student Alyson scored a 3 on alignment with professional standards, a 5 on the PowerPoint presentation, a 5 on historical background, and a 7 on edited copy for a composite rubric score of 20, she would earn a C for this project.

Now suppose that student Benjamin scored a 4 on alignment, a 6 on the PowerPoint, a 6 on historical background, and an 8 on edited copy. Although Benjamin's work fell into the same observable assessment criteria boxes on the matrix as did the work of Alyson, Benjamin received the higher of the two possible column scores in each instance. His composite rubric score would be a 24, earning him a B on this project.

Alyson would not learn anything from the assessment process in regard to what would need to be done to attain a higher score in each strand because the performance descriptor is the same for the two numerical values. Assigning a score becomes in part a subjective decision, not an observable criterion-based decision. Benjamin would not be sure why he received the higher of the two possible scores in each column and would not know what to keep doing in order to keep scoring at the same level. All students being assessed using this rubric would go into the process with a great deal of uncertainty, muttering a lot of variations on the theme of "What exactly does the instructor *want*?"

Implementing a rubric with a range of scores for each column also prevents an instructor from getting accurate pictures of how students are progressing. This would be true whether considering an individual student's work across a semester or considering the overall understanding of an entire class.

In short, using a range of scores as column headings invites the same problems pertaining to equity and fairness that rubric assessment was developed to dispel. If numerical values are to be assigned to rubric columns to reflect levels of performance, assign only one value per column and assign consecutive numbers that reflect the level of quality described in each column.

COMMON ERROR #5: INCLUDING INCONSISTENT CRITERIA IN ONE OR MORE COLUMNS

Including key criteria in one or more columns that are not addressed in each column or omitting a key criterion in one or more columns is usually, but not exclusively, a problem associated with holistic rubrics rather than analytic rubrics. The nature of analytic rubrics makes this easier to avoid; it is essentially one of the steps involved in analytic rubric design. When describing

Table 8.5. Prepare a Fifteen-Minute, Standards-Aligned PowerPoint Presentation Addressing the Historical Background of an American Political Party (20 Possible Points)

Criteria	0	1–2	3–4	5–6	7–8
Aligned with Professional Standards	Not aligned with standards	Indirectly aligned	Aligned with at least one standard	Directly aligned with at least one standard	Directly aligned with at least two standards
Fifteen-Minute PowerPoint Preparation	Not in PowerPoint format or exceeds the time limit	Ineffective design or sequencing of presentation	Effort to design and sequence the presentation is apparent	Effectively designed and sequenced presentation	Effectively designed and sequenced presentation, tech enhanced
Historical Background	Multiple inaccuracies or no use of secondary sources	Vague information or minor inaccuracies; used secondary sources	Accurate information; used five or fewer secondary sources	Accurate information; used more than five secondary sources	Accurate information; used more than five secondary sources and at least one primary source
Edited Copy	>7 typo, APA, or mechanical errors	6–7 typo, APA, or mechanical errors	4–5 typo, APA, or mechanical errors	2–3 typo, APA, or mechanical errors	0–1 typo, APA, or mechanical error

32–27 points = A; 26–21 points = B; 20–15 points = C; 14–9 points = D; Below 9 points = F performance objectives in narrative form, it is helpful to dissect the narrative into individual performance criteria. Strive for parallel construction and consistency of criteria to be considered for assessment purposes whether working with an analytic or a holistic rubric.

When working with holistic rubrics, the volume of information to be communicated in paragraph form makes it easier to miss components. This is especially applicable when the descriptions are presented in horizontal paragraphs of narrative descriptions, as is often the case with holistic rubrics.

Consider the example in table 8.6. The "unacceptable" level paints a picture of ineffective working communication and collaboration between the university and its relevant professional community. However, in doing so, no mention is made of involvement for other members of the professional community; the specific development of candidate knowledge, skills, and professional dispositions; or collaboration to provide professional development opportunities for candidates. These are all key components that are addressed in the "acceptable" level and further expanded in the "exceptional" level.

The first step in checking the alignment of information in paragraph form is to reformat the paragraphs into vertical columns so that key components

Table 8.6.   Rubric for Evaluating University and Professional Partner Interaction in Intern Field Experiences and Clinical Practice Placements (NCATE, 2008)

UNACCEPTABLE—The university makes decisions about interns' placements and grading independent of the site supervisor hosting them. The unit's professional partners have little or no participation in the design, delivery, or evaluation of field experiences or clinical practice. Securing field placements is solely the responsibility of the interns.

ACCEPTABLE—The university, site supervisors, and other members of the professional community design, deliver, and evaluate field experiences and clinical practice to help candidates develop their knowledge, skills, and professional dispositions. The unit and its professional partners jointly determine the specific placement of interns to provide appropriate learning experiences. The university and professional sites share expertise and collaborate in providing professional development opportunities to support candidates' learning in field experiences and clinical practice.

EXCEPTIONAL—The university, site supervisors, and other members of the professional community design, deliver, and evaluate field experiences and clinical practice to help candidates develop and determine potential areas of specific expertise pertaining to their knowledge, skills, and professional dispositions. The unit and its professional partners jointly determine the specific placement of interns to provide appropriate learning experiences for the interns and to maximize related benefits for the professional partners' clients. The university and professional sites share expertise and integrate resources to collaborate in providing professional development opportunities to support candidates' learning in field experiences and clinical practice and to enhance the professional development of personnel at the clinical site.

may be more easily tracked from one performance level to the next. Second, underline or highlight the key components in each column. Focusing on verbs (in boldface) used in the narrative descriptions will assist in this task, as demonstrated in table 8.7.

Table 8.7. Reformatted Rubric for Evaluating University and Professional Partner Interaction in Intern Field Experiences and Clinical Practice Placements

Unacceptable	*Acceptable*	*Exceptional*
The university **makes decisions** about interns' placements independent of the site supervisor hosting them. The unit's professional partners **have little or no participation** in the design, delivery, or evaluation of field experiences or clinical practice. **Securing field placements** is solely the responsibility of the interns.	The university, site supervisors, and other members of the professional community **design, deliver, and evaluate** field experiences and clinical practice to **help candidates develop** their knowledge, skills, and professional dispositions. The unit and its professional partners **jointly determine** the specific placement of interns **to provide** appropriate learning experiences. The university and professional sites **share expertise and collaborate** in providing professional development opportunities **to support** candidates' learning in field experiences and clinical practice.	The university, site supervisors, and other members of the professional community **design, deliver, and evaluate** field experiences and clinical practice to **help candidates develop and determine** potential areas of specific expertise pertaining to their knowledge, skills, and professional dispositions. The unit and its professional partners **jointly determine** the specific placement of interns **to provide** appropriate learning experiences for the interns and **to maximize** related benefits for the professional partners' clients. The university and professional sites **share expertise and integrate resources to collaborate** in providing professional development opportunities **to support** candidates' learning in field experiences and clinical practice and **to enhance** the professional development of personnel at the clinical site.

In this example, there are only three components addressed in the unacceptable level but five components mentioned in the acceptable level and six in the exceptional level. It would appear at first glance that there are seven components in the exceptional level, but "to help candidates develop and determine potential areas of expertise pertaining to their knowledge . . ." is an expansion of the component "to design, deliver, and evaluate field experiences" and not a stand-alone component.

The rubric can now be revised to ensure key components are addressed across columns, as was done in table 8.8. Reordering the sequence of components to be more uniform across columns, in this case moving the component of determining placements to the same position in all three narratives, also makes the components easier to follow across columns.

The revised rubric language could now be converted back into the horizontal paragraph format if desired. The resulting rubric can now be applied to every instance of university and professional partner interactions where these particular components have been identified as key in assessing their joint involvement in interns' field experiences and clinical practice placements. The rubric is strengthened because the same components are addressed across all rubric levels.

MINI CASE STUDY: RUBRIC REVISION

With these five common errors in mind, and building upon the design considerations of the ten basic steps in rubric construction presented in chapters 5 and 6, it is time for application of what has been learned. The rubric in table 8.9 is presented to provide practice in diagnosing and editing some of the common errors in rubric design.

The rubric was drafted in a college setting several years ago. The author was not involved in the rubric design process but was asked to help check the rubric for effectiveness and inter-rater reliability during the pilot phase of its implementation. The rubric was an assessment tool to be used in the evaluation of student work as part of a process related to ongoing accreditation at the state and national levels. The focal point of the assignment was to write a college-level essay on a content topic germane to the student's intended teaching area. Students were required to take a position and support it in their essay.

Errors in rubric design were noted during the initial full-scale pilot implementation of the rubric. Work through the rubric for essay evaluation in table 8.9, identifying any errors you can find and revising the rubric as needed to eliminate the errors. Use the key considerations section at the end of this

Table 8.8. Revised Rubric for Evaluating University and Professional Partner Interaction in Intern Field Experiences and Clinical Practice Placements

Unacceptable	Acceptable	Exceptional
The unit's professional partners have little or no participation in the design, delivery, or evaluation of field experiences or clinical practice to help candidates develop skills and professional dispositions. The university alone makes decisions about interns' placements to provide appropriate learning experiences. Securing field placements is solely the responsibility of the interns. The university and professional sites rarely or never share expertise and collaborate in providing professional development opportunities to support candidates' learning in field experiences and clinical practice. No collaboration exists to enhance the professional development of personnel at the clinical site.	The university, site supervisors, and other members of the professional community design, deliver, and evaluate field experiences and clinical practice to help candidates develop their knowledge, skills, and professional dispositions. The unit and its professional partners jointly determine the specific placement of interns to provide appropriate learning experiences for the interns. The university and professional sites share expertise and collaborate in providing professional development opportunities to support candidates' learning in field experiences and clinical practice. Little or no collaboration exists to enhance the professional development of personnel at the clinical site.	The university, site supervisors, and other members of the professional community design, deliver, and evaluate field experiences and clinical practice to help candidates develop and determine potential areas of specific expertise pertaining to their knowledge, skills, and professional dispositions. The unit and its professional partners jointly determine the specific placement of interns to provide appropriate learning experiences for the interns and to maximize related benefits for the professional partners' clients. The university and professional sites share expertise and integrate resources to collaborate in providing professional development opportunities to support candidates' learning in field experiences and clinical practice and to enhance the professional development of personnel at the clinical site.

Table 8.9. Rubric for Essay Evaluation

	Developing	Proficient	Accomplished
Thesis Statement	Presents an inadequate thesis statement and/or makes insufficent connections between the thesis and related ideas.	Presents an adequate thesis statement and makes sufficient connections between the thesis and related ideas. The theoretical base is a good fit for the content.	Presents an insightful thesis statement and draws strong connections between the thesis and related ideas. The theoretical base is an excellant fit for the content.
Thoroughness of Content Knowledge	The paper showed that the student ubderstood the topic and addressed some of the important areas related to the topic.	The paper showed the student reviewed the literature and demonstrated sufficient depth of content in the topic. The student analyzed and addressed the most important issues related to the topic and provided supporting details to indicate understanding of the most important issues.	The paper showed the student reviewed the literature and demonstrated outstanding depth of content in the topic. The student addressed the most important issues and other related sub-topics and provided supporting details to indicate understanding of the important issues.
Accuracy of Content Knowledge	Some of the content and the conclusions drawn were accurate, but some areas were vague or did not show an understanding of the accuracy of content.	The content in the paper was accurate. The content was analyzed and conclusions were logical. Overall, there was evidence of accurate, connected content knowledge.	The content in the paper was extensive in breadthand depth, Conclusions based on the information were logical and were based on accurate content. Insights into the content were accurately expressed.
Organization	Presents a poorly organized progression of ideas and supporting information	Presents a sufficiently organized progression of ideas and supporting information.	Presents a logical and clear progression of ideas and supporting information.
Synthesis of Information	Poorly sythesizes ideas from research sources, presenting limited supporting information relevant to the thesis.	Sufficiently synthesizes ideas from research sources and presents supporting information mostly relevant to the thesis.	Extensive synthesis of idesa from research sources and oresents detailed supporting information clearly relevant to the thesis.

Multiple Perspectives	Provides a limited number of perspectives. Few connections were made between and within topics and with candidate's own perspective.	Provides an adequate number of perspectives. Connections were made between and within topics and with candidate's own perspective.	Provides serveral different perspectives and demonstrates their relevance to the thesis. Extensive connections were made between and within topics and with candidate's own perspective.
Selection of Sourced	Chooses few recent sources and/ or chooses sources with little credibility.	Chooses an adequate number of recent sources, all with sufficient credibility.	Chooses multiple recent sources, all with excellent credibility.
Conclusion	Arrives at an insufficiently documented conclusion.	Arrives at a sufficiently documented conclusion based on the information presented.	Arrives at a well documented, Logical conclusion based on the information presented.
Citations and Bibliography	Inconsistently cites references within the paper using APA style correctly and/or demonstrates correct APA fomat for title page, pagination, and bibliography.	Generally cites references within the paper using APA style correctly and demonstrates, correct APA format for title page, pagination, and bibliography.	Consistently cites references within the paper using APA style correctly and demonstrates correct APA format for title page, bibliography.
Mechanics	Uses correct grammer, spelling, and/ or punctuation inconsistently.	Uses correct grammer, spelling, and/or punctuation in almost all instances.	Consistently uses correct grammer, spelling, and/or punctuation.

chapter to help you get started. Analysis of the errors and an edited version of the rubric may be found on subsequent pages.

Errors in the rubric in table 8.9 fell under aspects of the fourth, fifth, and sixth steps of rubric construction. If you have not already done so, before reading further or looking at the revised version of the rubric, take a pen or pencil and spend a few minutes editing or making notes in the margins. Errors are analyzed here by the step in which they would have occurred during the design process.

STEP 4 ERRORS

One aspect that could not be gleaned from perusing the rubric itself needs to be explained up front as it was observable only to individuals involved in the actual piloting of the rubric. Additional components or aspects of existing components that need to be added to the rubric often come to light during the piloting process, as was the case with this rubric. This is quite normal and happens more often than not.

For example, when assessing the first round of essays on the component of the thesis statement, readers found that it wasn't always a simple question of an inadequate, adequate, or insightful thesis statement. In some instances, students were not focusing on the thesis topic they had identified, omitted a thesis statement, or were attempting to address several topics in the same five-page essay. Any or all of these concerns could be symptomatic of not having a clear concept of what a thesis statement is and how it can function to support the narrative in a written essay. However, there was no means on the original rubric to address the concern of missing or multiple thesis statements or treatments. This was added to the revised copy.

Language addressing the theoretical base was removed as it was only present in two of the three existing columns. It appeared better suited to one of the strands pertaining to content—if it needed to be included at all, as its meaning was unclear. It is always a good idea to provide examples of what is meant if wording requiring a subjective value judgment (inadequate/adequate/insightful) must be used at all. If an experienced reader is having difficulty understanding why a given thesis statement was deemed to be insightful and not merely adequate, an inexperienced student author is also likely to be unsure.

Another concern that surfaced came in the component that addressed synthesis of information. One of the essays to be assessed contained extensive, broad, accurate content that was perfectly cited using flawless APA style. So what was the problem?

The student had stacked line after line of narrative consisting of beautifully documented quotes. The whole paper consisted of quotes, one right after the other—not an easy task—but there was no attempt at synthesis or original thought. Experienced readers could recall having seen this before. It is not common, but it needs to be caught, and any students doing this need redirection to find their own author voices. This change was also made in the revised rubric.

STEP 5 ERRORS

There were two revisions needed under construction step five, which pertains to selecting the number of rubric columns. The first was simply to add numbers to the columns, seeing as they were to be used for scoring purposes. The second was to add another column for the value of zero or a column for "Unsatisfactory," using the system of column descriptors already in place.

In several of the papers, the components to be assessed were simply not present, so a score of 1, or "Developing," was not appropriate. How can a component be said to be developing if it is not there? For example, in one paper there was no conclusion. In another there were no resources addressed. In the example in table 8.9, no synthesis had taken place. The fourth column was added in the revised rubric.

STEP 6 ERRORS

The sixth step deals with writing the observable assessment criteria for each intersection of criterion and rating. What can seem like a good idea at the time of writing a rubric, or seem like a term any reasonable person could be expected to understand, often does not play out that way and revisions are needed. This is usually the step at which most of the work takes place in rubric construction. It is the most time-consuming step in the design process. It is also usually the area in which the most revisions are made after a rubric is piloted, which was the case with the rubric in our mini case study.

Overall, the rubric was revised to use language that focused on the product to be produced rather than on what the student did or did not do. As mentioned in a previous chapter, one of the inherent strengths a rubric can bring to the assessment process is that it can provide an objective means to focus on the work rather than on the personalities of the professors or students involved. Language in most cells needed revision in order to place the focus on the content of the strand component.

Table 8.10. Rubric for Essay Evaluation Too

	Undeveloped 0	Developing 1	Proficient 2	Accomplished 3
Thesis Statement	Thesis statement missing or not connected to the actual thesis.	Thesis statement inadequate and/or insufficient connections between the thesis and related ideas.	Thesis statement adequate and sufficient connections between the thesis and related ideas.	Thesis statement insightful and strong connections drawn between the thesis and related ideas.
Thoroughness of Content Knowledge	Understanding of content not communicated in the essay or gaps in expected knowledge were evident.	Search of the literature appeared adequate. Understanding of the topic was communicated in the essay; some of the important areas related to the topic were addressed.	Search of the literature evidenced sufficient depth. The most important issues related to the topic were analyzed and addressed with supporting details.	Search of the literature demonstrated outstanding depth. The most important issues and other related subtopics were addressed with supporting details.
Accuracy of Content Knowledge	Inaccurate content, concerns regarding application of content knowledge, or content knowledge not included.	Some of the content was accurate, but some areas were vague or did not show accurate applications of the content knowledge.	The content was accurate and analyzed with connected or applied content knowledge.	The content was accurate and extensive in breadth and depth, well analyzed, with well-connected or applied insights into the content knowledge.
Organization	Progression of ideas and/or supporting information could not be located.	Progression of ideas and/or supporting information poorly organized.	Progression of ideas and/or supporting information sufficiently organized.	Progression of ideas and/or supporting information logically and clearly organized.
Synthesis of Information	Ideas from research sources missing or cannot be identified.	Ideas from research sources poorly synthesized with limited supporting information relevant to the thesis.	Ideas from research sources sufficiently synthesized with supporting information mostly relevant to the thesis.	Ideas from research sources extensively synthesized with detailed supporting information clearly relevant to the thesis.

Criteria				
Multiple Perspectives	Multiple perspectives missing, not related to thesis topic, or not connected with each other or candidate's own perspective(s).	At least two perspectives included, perhaps related directly to thesis topic; connections were made between perspectives and with candidate's own perspective(s).	At least three if not four perspectives included, most related directly to the thesis topic; connections were made between perspectives and with candidate's own perspective(s).	At least four if not more perspectives included and related directly to the thesis topic; extensive connections were made between perspectives and with candidate's own perspective(s).
Selection of Sources	No sources included or concerns regarding credibility of sources.	Few (<3) recent sources and/or sources with little credibility.	An adequate number (3–5) of recent sources, all with sound credibility.	Multiple (>5) recent sources, all with sound credibility.
Conclusion	No conclusion documented.	Conclusion insufficiently documented or not based on information presented.	Conclusion sufficiently documented and based on information presented.	Logical conclusion well documented and based on information presented.
APA Citations in Text and Reference List	No references within the paper or in a reference list at the end of the paper.	References within the paper and reference list reflect APA style with several errors; one or more reference(s) may appear in one place but not the other.	References within the paper and reference list reflect APA style with some errors; all references appear in both places.	References within the paper and reference list reflect APA style with few or no errors; all references appear in both places.
APA Format	Missing title page or pagination (headings optional).	APA format used for title page, pagination, and headings with errors.	APA format correctly used for title page, pagination, and headings with minor errors.	APA format correctly used for title page, pagination, and headings.
APA Mechanics	Concerns regarding two or more areas: grammar, spelling, and punctuation.	Correct grammar, spelling, and/or punctuation inconsistently used.	Correct grammar, spelling, and/or punctuation used with minor errors.	Correct grammar, spelling, and/or punctuation consistently used.

As a starting point for considering individual strands, in the strand for "Selection of Sources," a quantity-structured approach provided a less vague term than "multiple." This resulted in a more equitable means to apply the rubric. When reviewing essays that had been previously scored by another reader, one essay was spotted wherein the writer had used three resources and earned a score of 3 on that rubric strand while another essay with eight resources, of comparable or better quality, had only been scored with a 1.

Clearly there was a good deal of uncertainty regarding the interpretation of "multiple." Numerical values in the column heading would provide a more objective basis for assigning a score in that strand. Suggested numerical values were included in the revised cells.

The strand for citations and bibliography (which should be called "References" if APA style is in use) was found to benefit from increased specificity or conversion to two strands, both of which were done in the revision. One essay with application errors on the cover page and errors in the reference list had scored a 2, yet another with a flawless APA cover page and hardly any errors in the reference list had also received a 2. The basis for scoring was not clear and was revised.

Another clarity issue involved an instance where components were included in more than one strand. This is not a problem if more than one strand is used to address different aspects of a component. This was not the case, and if it was the intent, the difference was not clear. There was a separate component strand set up for "Conclusion" where it would be expected, toward the end of the rubric.

The element of conclusions was also scrambled into the middle of the cells under the criterion "Accuracy of Content Knowledge." This disrupted the flow of the cell language and put too much information into one cell. The duplication was removed in the revision.

As noted in the previous chapter, it is important to model what is expected in terms of correct spelling, grammar, mechanics, punctuation, and so on. This is especially the case when the rubric assesses for accuracy in the area where an error is made—for example, when a word is misspelled in the strand that targets spelling. The multiple errors in spelling, spacing, and capitalization were corrected in the revised version.

Another APA violation, that of anthropomorphism or attaching animate capabilities to inanimate objects, is often a mark of inexperienced writers. The second strand included "the paper showed . . ." phrasing. This was removed in the revised version of the rubric.

A full version of the revised rubric may be found in table 8.10. To get a clear picture of the revisions and the reasons for them, it may be helpful to make a photocopy of the revised version and compare it with the original draft in table 8.9. There may be changes with which you do not agree or, on the other hand, that you feel did not go far enough. That is to be expected. The revision process is an individual one and preferred cell language will often differ from person to person. However, the reasons underlying the changes are sound and worth considering as you work to avoid or edit out similar errors in your own assessment rubrics.

In summary, there are several factors to consider when designing rubrics that will help to prevent common errors in rubric design. The points in this chapter are summarized in the following set of key considerations that may be useful in circumventing mistakes frequently made when undertaking rubric design.

KEY CONSIDERATIONS: WAYS TO AVOID COMMON ERRORS IN RUBRIC DESIGN

- Avoid subjective or values-based terms such as "good" or "exemplary" when writing rubric descriptors. (These terms can work as column headings but not as strand descriptors.)
- Use specific descriptive language in cells to avoid the trap of a Likert scale in a matrix.
- Omit rubric strands that are contextual requirements (e.g., hue of the section dividers) but nonessential to determining the quality of the performance or product to be assessed.
- If a strand reflects a key component more essential to the quality of the final product or performance than the other strands, consider weighting the element to emphasize its importance.
- Avoid using a range of numbers when assigning numerical values to rubric columns—assign only one value per column, in consecutive order.
- Be sure the same criteria are addressed in each column across rubric strands. (This tends to be more of a concern in holistic rubrics but can also be a concern in analytic rubrics.)
- Check alignment of multiple criteria across columns when formatting holistic rubrics.
- Carefully check spelling, grammar, punctuation, parallel construction, and the like.
- Revise your rubric drafts and expect to engage in problem solving if challenges arise during implementation.

IMPLEMENTING RUBRIC ASSESSMENTS

9

Converting Rubric Scores to Grades

One of the most common concerns expressed by newcomers to rubric use is how to convert rubric scores to percentage scores or to traditional letter grades. After all, if the highest possible rubric point total is 27, it would not do to provide that numerical score on an individual assignment or as a course grade to a student accustomed to the traditional 100% as the desired score. Seeing a 27 without benefit of some clear explanation may result in cardiac arrest, cardio exercise, or carb overload, depending on if the student's stress reaction of choice is panic, working out, or pigging out. (If the lap pool is closed, don't ask what the author's second choice option would be and keep the chocolate coming.)

Context for any numerical score is critical. As a high school student, the author somehow missed the fact that the top score on the SAT sections was 800, whereas the best possible ACT score was a 36. Receiving an ACT score report close to 30 brought the ubiquitous test taker's nightmare come true of being "off by one" when filling in those little circles with a number-two pencil. When a friend shared her score and seemed happy about scoring close to 30, it raised the question of why she too was not hiding in her room. After a couple expletives pertaining to wondering how someone who scored close to 30 could possibly be so clueless in this matter, she explained the ACT grading system.

Why devote a paragraph in an academic book to that story? It was done to emphasize the importance of context when it comes to grading systems. Students will be a lot more comfortable with rubric assessment, or any kind of assessment for that matter, if explanations and examples of how rubrics may be applied are clear, well organized, and readily available. This is especially important if your students are either encountering rubric assessment for the first time or have had some bad experiences with it.

Some students are initially uncertain about rubric assessment due to prior experiences with rubrics involving nebulous conversion systems, too much leeway in column values, or other surprises of a nonpositive nature. Clear explanations in the syllabus and examples provided in class or in an online course room can assure students that the rubric assessment system the instructor plans to implement is equitable and consistent. Well-designed rubrics can alleviate, rather than exacerbate, concerns about what to expect in regard to assessment and grading.

The task of converting rubric scores to percentages or letter grades is actually very easy to accomplish. There are three main scenarios where this is required: (1) converting rubric score point totals on an individual assignment to a percentage or letter grade for that assignment, (2) converting rubric score point totals on major papers or projects completed during a course to a letter grade for the course, and (3) combining rubric score point totals and other forms of scoring, such as traditional percentages, to a letter grade for an entire course.

CONVERTING A RUBRIC SCORE
ON AN ASSIGNMENT TO A LETTER GRADE

The simplest means of converting a rubric score on an individual assignment is to do some simple mathematics and list the grade equivalents or create a table with the results. For example, if a rubric contains five strands, with a possibility of zero to four points per strand, the rubric contains 20 possible points. If a traditional grading system is followed, 93% to 100% translates to an A, 86% to 92% translates to a B, and so on. Using this same system, 93% of 20 points is 18.60. If this is rounded up, the whole number score would be 19. So in order to earn an A on this assignment, the student can only miss one point and needs to score a 4 on every strand but one. That is mathematically correct—but does it accurately describe the parameters of the performance needed for an A on the rubric?

In a five-column rubric, such as the one in table 9.1 with the lowest score on the left and the highest on the right, the far right column is usually reserved for descriptions of exemplary work. In letter grade terms, it is the A+ column. In percentage terms, an A+ is 97% to 100%. So in order to earn an A+ on this assignment, a student must rate a perfect score of 20. A 19 would earn an A. And a 17 or 18—which would mean a score of 4 or A+ on one or two of the strands and a 3 or A on the other three or four strands—would earn a B. Wait

Table 9.1. Assessment Rubric: Research Paper—Administrator Interview

Component	0	1	2	3	4
Administrator Selected for Interview	Administrator has not supervised faculty	←	Administrator no longer has supervisory responsibilities	↑	Administrator has current supervisory responsibilities
Interview Protocol Followed	Protocol not followed	Missing more than 1 protocol question	Missing all or part of 1 of the protocol questions	Protocol followed	Protocol followed; additional and/or follow-up questions added
Field Note Summary	Missing or not following format on 2 or more components	Missing or not following format on one component	All components but questions and summation of responses do not follow format	All components but missing components of introductory paragraph	Complete introductory paragraph, all questions with summary of responses, reflection paragraph
Observation/Assessment Instrument(s)	Missing an attached copy of observation/assessment instrument(s)	Blank copy of instrument(s) that could be used is/are attached to matrix	Blank copy of instrument(s) used is/are attached to field note summary matrix	Partially completed instrument(s) attached to field note summary matrix	Fully completed instrument(s) attached to field note summary matrix
Edited Copy	>7 typo, APA, or mechanical errors	6–7 typo, APA, or mechanical errors	4–5 typo, APA, or mechanical errors	2–3 typo, APA, or mechanical errors	0–1 typo, APA, or mechanical errors

a minute . . . does the simple mathematical answer fit the question of what rubric profiles align with performance levels of an A or a B?

In some cases, the simple mathematical formula might work. However, when using a rubric to score an individual assignment, it is never a given and it usually doesn't work. That is especially the case when working with a rubric that contains multiple columns and that includes a column to rate strand characteristics as exemplary.

Is the answer to design six-column rubrics with a column for each traditional letter grade and an extra column for an A+? What works better is to get away from percentage calculations and formulaic approaches to numerical scores. Establish letter-grade equivalents that fit the rubric cell descriptions and the individual assessment task for which the rubric was developed.

A means of thinking through the fit between rubric point total and overall performance rating is to consider all of the possible strand score combinations in terms of what would or would not fit with an overall letter-grade performance, as was done in table 9.2.

Based on the possible combinations in table 9.2, combinations totaling 16–20 points would appear to fit with the letter grade of A. The rubric designer may not be comfortable with even one rubric strand score of a 1 or 2 factoring into the point total for an A. If that is the case, a footnote could include the information that a composite rubric score with a strand score lower than a 2 or a 3 would not equate to an A and the project would receive a letter grade of B.

Table 9.2.   Strand Score Combinations for Rubric in Table 9.1

Option	0	1	2	3	4	Total Points
A					5×4 (20)	20
B				1×3 (3)	4×4 (16)	19
C			1×2 (2)		4×4 (16)	18
D				2×3 (6)	3×4 (12)	18
E		1×1 (1)			4×4 (16)	17
F			1×2 (2)	1×3 (3)	3×4 (12)	17
G				3×3 (9)	2×4 (8)	17
H		1×1 (1)			4×4 (16)	17
I		2×2 (4)			3×4 (12)	16
J		1×2 (2)		2×3 (6)	2×4 (8)	16
K				4×3 (12)	1×4 (4)	16
L				1×3 (3)	3×4 (12)	15
M		2×2 (4)		1×3 (3)	2×4 (8)	15
N		1×1 (1)		2×3 (6)	2×4 (8)	15
O			1× (2)	3×3 (9)	1×4 (4)	15
P				5×3 (15)		15

The strand point combinations do not have a set rule or formula to follow for what equates to a letter grade. Let the needs of the assessment determine the design rules. Rely on how well the different cell combinations describe a performance level that you as the rubric developer believe equates to a given letter grade for the performance described in an individual rubric.

CONVERTING A RUBRIC SCORE ON AN ASSIGNMENT TO A PERCENTAGE

Connecting rubric scores with final semester percentages involves letting the desired percentage points for the individual assignments provide the alignment point for the rubric score rather than aligning the raw scores to percentages. For example, some online courses are organized so that the points for all of the projects within a course add up to 100. A project with an assessment rubric like that in table 9.1, in which the highest possible number of rubric points is 20, would be easy to align with a project worth 20 percent of the course grade. It would also be easy to align with the percentage if the project were worth 10 percent. When designing a rubric for an assignment worth a preestablished percentage of the total course points, it is helpful to make the conversion a simple ratio of 1:1, 2:1, or the like.

If the number of strands and columns cannot be aligned using a simple ratio, a mathematical approach can be effective. For example, how could the project grade be determined if the rubric in table 9.1 assessed a project worth 15 percent of the course grade instead of 10 or 20 percent? The percentage score of 15 would be divided by 20. The resulting quotient of .75 would be multiplied by the number of rubric points attained. If a student earned 18 out of 20 points, and the assignment being scored is worth 15 percent of the total course grade, the instructor would multiply the number of points earned (18) by .75. The student would have attained 13.5 percent of the possible 15 percent of the total course grade that the individual assignment is worth.

CONVERTING RUBRIC SCORES ON ALL COURSE ASSIGNMENTS TO A COURSE PERCENTAGE OR LETTER GRADE

Although the simple mathematical approach to rubric score conversions is not usually effective with individual assignments, it is often very effective when computing a final percentage or letter grade for all major projects completed in a course. This involves starting with the number of possible points for all major course projects or assignments, adding them to obtain a course composite, and determining the percentages or letter grade equivalents. For example, if there are 116 total points possible in all the rubrics for all of the assignments or projects used to determine the composite point total for a course, two possible scoring conversions would be as outlined in table 9.3. Here are the course assignments with possible rubric point totals:

1. Improvement Plan Supervision Project (36 points)
2. Action Research Paper (20 points)
3. Mid-Term Case Study Analysis (20 points)
4. Online Discussion and Participation (24 points)
5. Final Philosophy and Reflection (16 points)

Commercial course assessment systems, such as Taskstream or LiveText, provide ways to design and score rubrics electronically. Individual student scores, running totals, and class statistics are available with only a few mouse clicks. Students and instructors have access to rubrics and rubric scores as soon as the latter are posted.

In most systems, the aggregate values are maintained by assignment: tracking the actual breakdown of the points by strand may not be a system option. It may be helpful, for purposes of fine-tuning assignments for subsequent classes and monitoring student performance on the strand-specific components of assignments, to develop a system for maintaining your own strand scores, as demonstrated in the matrix in table 9.4.

This can be done on a spreadsheet, using Excel or similar software. It can also be done with a simple table. As experienced instructors know, maintaining a copy of student scores is invaluable in the remote chance a campus-based system crashes. It may also be difficult if not impossible to access individual student assignment scores in a campus data system after the semester ends.

Maintaining your own set of student scores, coded by course number and any other identifying criteria you find helpful, is also a good idea if a student should challenge a grade. Of course, if you are using well-designed and well-

Table 9.3. Course Grade Conversion Options

Letter Grade	Percentage Option 1	Rubric Points	Percentage Option 2	Rubric Points
A	90% to 100%	104–116	93% to 100%	108–116
B	80% to 89%	93–103	85% to 92%	99–107
C	70% to 79%	81–92	77% to 84%	89–98
D	60% to 69%	70–80	70% to 76%	81–88

Table 9.4. Sample Class Composite Rubric Score Table

Course Code: _____   Semester: _____

Student Names	Discussion and Participation	Research Paper	Supervision Project	Midterm Case Study	Final Philosophy and Reflection	Total Rubric Points	Letter Grade
Student 1	22	4 4 4 4 4	4 4 4 4 4 4 4 4 4	20	16	114	A
Student 2	20	4 3 4 4 3	4 2 4 4 3 3 4 4 4	20	16	106	B
Student 3	22	4 3 4 4 4	4 4 4 4 4 4 4 4 4	20	16	114	A
Student 4	24	4 4 4 4 4	2 4 4 3 4 4 4 4 4	20	16	113	A
Student 5	20	4 3 1 4 4	4 4 3 4 4 4 4 4 2	15	16	100	B
Student 6	22	4 3 4 4 4	4 4 3 4 4 4 4 4 4	18	16	110	A
Student 7	24	4 4 4 4 2	2 4 4 3 4 4 4 4 4	19	16	110	A

implemented rubrics, you will hopefully not need to maintain records for this purpose. But better safe than unprepared.

As the reader has probably noticed, the table 9.4 includes two major assignments, the research paper (rubric provided in table 9.1) and the supervision project, that were scored with rubrics. The other assignments were not.

The twelve online discussion postings were worth a maximum of two points per discussion: two points for a substantive post and a substantive response to another class member's post (examples of what did and did not constitute "substantive" were provided to students), one point if only one of the two components was enacted, and zero points if the student did not post or respond in the time frame allotted.

The final philosophy/reflection assignment was drafted in this particular course and the final copy—scored with a rubric—was produced in the last course of the degree program. The only way not to earn 16 points was not to complete and submit the assignment.

The midterm case study in this example was analyzed and written up in teams. Although a rubric was used to assess the case study, it was not deemed necessary to record strand scores. Only the total number of rubric points was recorded on the composite matrix for the case study.

Actually two rubrics were used in connection with the case study. The first was a traditional rubric on which the bottom strand was used to assess the student's contributions to the group project. Students may not care for group assignments if they have ever been part of a less-than-functional group, did all the work, or worked with someone in the group who was not a dependable team member.

It has already been noted that rubrics can be helpful self-assessment tools. They can also be helpful in providing team members with a means to assess the quality of other team members' contributions as well as their own. When scoring group work or team projects with a rubric, all team members could complete a rubric similar to the assessment instrument in table 9.5.

It would not be practical for students to submit these rubrics anonymously, but only the instructor would see them. Each member's scores for the other team or group members are kept confidential between student and instructor. An average of members' score as provided by group or team colleagues is computed, rounding up if necessary. Students would know their contribution was perceived by their team members as less than optimal if they receive a less-than-optimal score on this rubric strand.

That being said, a combined rating on one rubric strand will not be enough to derail a student's project score in the event of toxic working relationships within the group if all other strands receive strong ratings. Citing clear expectations for group participation and using them for scoring purposes can

Table 9.5. Group Work Assessment Rubric: Mid-Term Case Study

Component	0	1	2	3	4
Contribution to Team Project* Name:	Contributions inconsistent, late or not produced, do not meet group's quality standards, or provided in a negative manner	One of four contribution components strong	Two of four contribution components strong	Three of four contribution components strong	Contributions are consistent, timely, high quality, and provided in a positive manner.
Contribution to Team Project* Name:	Contributions inconsistent, late or not produced, do not meet group's quality standards, or provided in a negative manner	One of four contribution components strong	Two of four contribution components strong	Three of four contribution components strong	Contributions are consistent, timely, high quality, and provided in a positive manner.
Contribution to Team Project* Name:	Contributions inconsistent, late or not produced, do not meet group's quality standards, or provided in a negative manner	One of four contribution components strong	Two of four contribution components strong	Three of four contribution components strong	Contributions are consistent, timely, high quality, and provided in a positive manner.
Contribution to Team Project* Name:	Contributions inconsistent, late or not produced, do not meet group's quality standards, or provided in a negative manner	One of four contribution components strong	Two of four contribution components strong	Three of four contribution components strong	Contributions are consistent, timely, high quality, and provided in a positive manner.

Note: Please check one matrix box for each team member named in the left-hand column. Remember to rate your own contribution. (Explanations may be made below, if necessary.)

communicate that these are not suggestions but expectations for contributions. This alone can alleviate some of the grading concerns that may arise with group or team projects. Students have observed that having a copy of the group contribution rubric prior to beginning work and knowing it will be used to determine one of the rubric strand scores has improved the overall level of everyone's contributions.

Whatever the systems that are developed and used for converting rubric strand scores to percentages or letter grades, it is essential that the systems are equitable and consistent. Take time at the beginning of the course to describe how the scores resulting from clear, well-organized, readily available rubrics will be converted to percentages or letter grades. Provide examples of how the rubrics will be scored and how the scores earned will impact individual assignment scores and the final composite grade in the course. The key considerations for this chapter provide a summary of points to keep in mind regarding rubric scores and grade conversions.

KEY CONSIDERATIONS: CONVERTING RUBRIC SCORES TO LETTER OR PERCENTAGE GRADES

Converting a rubric score on an individual assignment:

- Simple mathematics can be used to list percentage or letter-grade equivalents; however, establishing letter-grade equivalents that fit the rubric cell descriptions may be more effective, especially if the top column equates to an A+ level.
- Create a rubric points-to-percentage or points-to-letter-grade conversion table.
- Consider all possible strand score combinations when determining grade equivalents.
- A useful option is to restrict minimal values within a point combination.
- Strand point combinations do not have a set letter grade rule or formula to follow.
- Rely on how well point totals describe a performance level equating to a letter grade.
- When designing rubrics for assignments worth a preestablished percentage of the total course points, it is helpful to make conversions simple ratios of 1:1, 2:1, or the like.

Converting a composite of several rubric scores, or combinations of rubric scores and points from assignments assessed via other means, to a final course grade:

- Simple mathematical percentage approaches are often very effective when computing a final percentage or letter grade for all major projects completed in a course.
- It is helpful to develop a system for maintaining your own strand scores as well as project or course composite scores in case of system failure or campus archiving or eliminating electronic grade books soon after the end of the semester.

10

Designing a Standards-Aligned Rubric

The key to constructing a standards-aligned rubric is to use the standards to develop the descriptors that determine the rubric strands. Sets of professional standards at the local, state, or national levels are often organized with an overriding standard that is broken out into bulleted lists of specific elements, functions, skills, or expected professional competencies. If these are provided, it facilitates the work of the rubric developer because the observable attributes can easily be turned into descriptors for use in a performance-focused or product-focused rubric.

Good as the provided descriptors can be, accrediting bodies often encourage member organizations to add to them. This provides some college- or university-specific means in which candidates are expected to demonstrate standards-aligned competence. The practice helps prevent any tendency toward generic or "cookie cutter" programs that adhere simply to minimal standards or look pretty much the same from one institution to the next. It also helps schools find ways to implement requirements intended to distinguish their graduates, equipping them with unique skills or experiences as they enter the professional realm.

Program graduates or community partners can provide valuable perspectives when designing standards-aligned rubrics to assess preprofessional competence. Maintaining interactive working relationships with professionals in the local and online community can help to ensure graduates are prepared to meet the current demands of professional practice.

Field-based practitioners are often uniquely positioned to help determine the competencies that need to be demonstrated, especially when candidates are in field experiences or capstone internships. This was the case at a school where the author served in an administrative faculty position. The mini case study below took place within the context of an education school unit, but the approach taken can be applied in any field where substantive practitioner input is desired to accomplish the following goal. That goal was to design a rubric that aligns national and state standards with expected professional competencies, pertinent to both performance-related skills and professional artifacts, to be demonstrated by program graduates. *(Step 1 in rubric design: identify the goal of the assessment task and whether it involves processes, products, or both.)*

EXAMPLE 1: MINI CASE STUDY—COLLABORATIVE DEVELOPMENT OF A STANDARDS-BASED ASSESSMENT RUBRIC

Schools or departments of education are required to follow program graduates as they move into their initial positions to assess their preparation to work as entry-level professionals. This requirement is by no means confined to the professional-preparation programs in education. Data on how graduates perform and what impact their work has on clients is required in multiple fields and can be gathered from multiple sources.

One of the best sources is the employers of program graduates. Information gathered in this manner provides valuable data for ongoing program evaluation and revision. It can also be used to shape applied competency development for students while still in programs.

In this particular case, surveys sent to graduates' employers in the education unit had previously involved general items scored on a Likert scale. Likert-scale systems make surveys easy to complete and process, but they do not provide much if any specific feedback on knowledge and skills demonstrated by program graduates. Furthermore, Likert-scale ratings tend to be subjective: one rater's three can easily be another rater's five.

A standards-based instrument that asked for open-ended narrative feedback under each standard had also been tried. This attempt to elicit more direct and specific feedback resulted in a low return rate. Some of the forms that were returned were only partially completed or contained a note of apology stating that the form took too long to complete.

Another approach was needed. The decision was made to try developing a rubric. An instrument was needed that could offer ease of completion similar to that of a Likert scale. It also needed to provide specific feedback about the applied knowledge and skills demonstrated by program graduates. *(Step 2 in rubric design: be sure a rubric is an effective, efficient assessment option.)*

The faculty opted for an analytic rubric to assess the competence levels of our program graduates. *(Step 3 in rubric design: choose between an analytic or a holistic rubric.)* It was an easy choice because they wanted to focus on individual components of skills or applied knowledge related to each of the standards.

To begin work on this endeavor, a team was formed consisting of three college department members and six school-based professionals. Faculty members were asked to provide the names of experienced school administrators at the elementary-, middle-, and secondary-school levels whose schools had partnership agreements in place with the institution. Two principals were chosen from each level. All were honored to be invited to participate, and a mutually workable date to schedule a daylong meeting on campus was found.

Everyone was provided with a packet of preparatory material, including a sample rubric and a concise version of the state's professional teaching standards. Modeled very closely on the Interstate Teacher Assessment and Support Consortium (INTASC) standards, this standard set listed eleven "umbrella" competencies. Whereas the INTASC standards broke the umbrella standards out into expectations regarding skills, knowledge, and dispositions, the state standards focused solely on knowledge and skills.

This was probably done at least in part because dispositions are so difficult to objectively assess. It is possible to assess behaviors stemming from the acquisition of specific dispositions, as mentioned in the first section of this book. However, this can be a nebulous area in terms of legal accountability, and some states have chosen to address dispositions indirectly, if at all, when designing professional standards. Therefore, the team's preliminary step toward designing the rubric strand components was to obtain the most recent copy of the standards and the accompanying descriptors that addressed skills and knowledge to be evaluated.

Before reviewing the state professional standard set used in this case study, team members were asked to compile lists of the top ten or so components that were "must sees" in terms of a successful beginning teacher's work. What skills needed to be demonstrated by the time a beginner approaches the end of the first year? This was done to ensure that the knowledge base of practice was brought to the table and did not inadvertently slip through the cracks of preexisting state standards.

When the team met on campus for the first work session, members were asked to transfer the items on their lists to Post-it notes. One page of poster paper for each of the eleven state standards was put up on the walls with the standard and number written across the top of the page. A sheet was also posted for "Other," and the team would eventually determine which standard would best fit the handful of Post-its that ended up there. It did not take long for team members to write out the components they needed to see in order to recommend offering a beginning teacher a contract for a second year and attach them to one of the posters. *(Step 4 in rubric design: determine the row strand components to be assessed.)*

Team members were then divided into subgroups consisting of a college faculty member, a secondary administrator, and an elementary administrator. It was decided to use a five-strand rubric so that the middle column could be the minimal expectation for a beginning competence level. *(Step 5 in rubric design: select the number of columns and their descriptors and/or numerical ratings.)* The two columns on either side would permit the description of behaviors or products associated with levels of "very good" and "excellent" or "not quite there yet but working on it" and "competence not what it needs to be in this strand."

Perhaps a five-column rubric was chosen because the design team members were all educators and accustomed to an A/Excellent, B/Very Good, C/Average, D/Poor, F/You-Don't-Want-an-F approach to assessment? Descriptors similar to those were actually discussed. It was decided not to use them, mostly to avoid the punitive implications of an F on the rubric. The traditional D/Poor also did not reflect the working-on-it-but-not-where-it-needs-to-be spirit intended to be conveyed in the second column.

The team then had a long discussion about numerical ratings for the column headings—should zero to four or one to five be used? The latter was chosen. What was the rationale? By the time a beginning professional started that first position, there would hopefully not be any areas of competence that were not demonstrated at all.

The team could have gone with either option. What the reader will hopefully take away from this description is the importance of having these kinds of conversations. Collaboration in the assessment instrument development process has been said to be messy, and it does take more time than designing a rubric, or doing most things, on one's own. But in cases where the synergy of the group can be facilitated, the whole quickly becomes greater than the sum of its parts, and the finished product—in this case the rubric—benefits from the combined effects of everyone's best thinking.

Once the simple one-to-five column descriptors were selected, each group was then assigned three or four of the Post-it-covered poster sheets along with the task of developing rubric strands in five columns for each of their standards. *(Step 6 in rubric design: draft the observable assessment criteria for each cell in every strand.)*

The phase of the project in which rubric strands were developed took much longer than anticipated, approximately three and a half hours rather than the two hours that had originally been allotted. By midafternoon, everyone had worked extremely hard. Professional trust and camaraderie had quickly developed, and conversations had been intense at times. It was the original intent to limit practitioners' involvement to one meeting so they would not feel overly inconvenienced as a result of their involvement. This concern was quickly dispelled when administrators responded positively to the idea of reviewing the work in progress once the rubric drafts were typed into matrixes. They asked when the team could meet again to engage in further expansion of the original draft.

Group members subsequently devoted significant amounts of time to the project between meetings. A follow-up e-mail discussion on the use of the rubric led to a standard-by-standard discussion of the rubric strands when the group reconvened. The standards functioned as section headings, and no additional headings were deemed necessary. *(Step 7 in rubric design: decide whether or not headings would be helpful to organize the rubric.)*

The department chair had compared the initial draft with the knowledge and skill sections of each state standard and had added some strands. Design team members had also made extensive changes to wording and had developed additional strands. It was determined that no special weighting would be needed for any of the strands, as all were equally important. *(Step 8 in rubric design: add weightings, if appropriate, to augment column numerical ratings.)* Design team members had discovered that quite a bit of duplication existed between standards, which complicated the task somewhat. It was stated at one point, as members deliberated under which standard to place a new strand, that "the most important thing is that we have it, not where it is."

As has been addressed previously in this book, the design team found the rubric could serve multiple purposes. In addition to program evaluation, strands on the rubric instrument could provide college faculty with a basis for discussion, providing assistance, and setting goals or developing action plans if a beginning professional was struggling. Faculty members felt that the rubric could also be used by beginners as a self-assessment tool, providing a starting point for reflective analysis of one's own performance.

Administrators on the design team shared working drafts with teachers—including union members—for feedback and piloted the rubric with volunteers in their buildings. *(Step 9 in rubric design: pilot the rubric and revise as needed.)* One of the administrators on the design team shared a working draft of the rubric with personnel in his district who were responsible for designing the instruments used for assessment purposes. He felt what had been developed was more comprehensive, more behavior specific, and better able to be used for formative as well as summative assessment than what was currently used in his district.

Team members then made practical suggestions about the format of the rubric. It was decided to add a small line under each strand title where the score in each strand could be marked. It was felt this would diminish the

Table 10.1 Sample Rubric Sections from Standards-Aligned Graduate Follow-Up Rubric

State Standard #7: Communication

Score: Level:	1	2	3	4	5
1. Models accurate, effective communication	Concerns regarding written, spoken, or nonverbal communication: little or no attempt to improve.	Concerns regarding written, spoken, or nonverbal communication: working to improve.	Models basic skills in written, spoken, and nonverbal communication: working to improve.	Effectively, accurately models two of the three, working to improve basic skill in the third.	Effectively, accurately models written, spoken, and nonverbal communication.
2. Can guide team or group processes	Still learning group facilitation, listening, and conflict resolution.	Proficient in one of the three skill areas, working on other two.	Proficient in two of the three skill areas, working on the third.	Proficient in listening, group facilitation, and conflict resolution.	Proficient in all three skill areas; beginning ability to coach these skills in others.
3. Provides specific feedback to students	Provides negative or unhelpful feedback to students.	Provides positive but nonspecific feedback.	Occasionally provides specific feedback to all students.	Working to consistently provide specific feedback to all students.	Consistently provides specific feedback with improvement suggestions.

State Standard #8: Assessment

Score: Rating:	1	2	3	4	5
1. Implements different assessment techniques	Relies upon one kind of assessment or does not address assessment.	Assesses students at basic knowledge level.	Assesses knowledge and application of knowledge.	Assesses knowledge and application, beginning to assess integration of knowledge.	Matches assessment to learning outcomes desired; addresses knowledge, application, and integration.

Criteria					
2. Integrates assessment and instruction	Assessment has little or no impact on instruction or pacing of content.	Recognizes problems as result of assessment; often unsure what to do.	Attempts some intervention strategies, based on assessment.	Modifies instructional approach for most students, based on assessment.	Consistently modifies instruction for all students, based on assessment.
3. Uses assessment to address learning modalities	Students' learning modalities not used when determining assessment approaches.	Relies primarily upon one modality when assessing.	Proficient with assessment in one modality; beginning to experiment with two.	Proficient with assessment in one modality; beginning to experiment with all three.	Consistently uses verbal, written, and performance modalities when assessing.
4. Adapts assessments for students with special needs	Assessment perspective is one-size-fits-all.	Recognizes necessity to adapt assessments for students with special needs; developing basic skills in the three areas.	Can adapt assessments for students with one kind of special need; working to develop basic skill in other areas.	Can adapt assessments for students from two areas of special need; working to develop basic skills in third area.	Can adapt assessments for students with disabilities, from different cultural backgrounds, and with different primary languages.
5. Uses technology for assessment purposes	Does not yet use technology for assessment purposes.	Experiments with technology in assessment on a limited basis.	Uses technology to complete teacher-focused assessment tasks.	Uses technology for teacher-focused assessment tasks, beginning to involve students and parents.	Uses technology for teacher-focused assessment tasks; consistently involves students and parents.

chance of someone marking a graduate on the line between two categories as if on a continuum.

It was also decided to attach a separate half-page tear-off sheet where respondents could complete demographic information. When the survey was returned, it would be assigned a numerical code. The top sheet could then be removed and kept in a separate file to provide documentation of its return without compromising confidentiality of the respondents.

The resulting draft of the rubric, one page for each of the standards, was circulated to additional constituent groups on and off campus. It also received positive reviews from members of the campus-based committee whose approval was needed prior to launching a new assessment. *(Step 10 in rubric design: implement the rubric.)*

Academic units involved in the preparation of beginning professionals have always welcomed information on the performance of their graduates. The design team in this case study had developed a performance-based, rubric-format, survey instrument grounded in the state's professional practice standards. It was constructed from the primary perspectives of experienced professionals who brought many years of expertise in working with beginners. The result was a standards-aligned observable performance rubric to elicit specific feedback on what graduates demonstrated they knew and were able to do. A sample of the rubric, addressing standards 7 and 8, may be found in table 10.1.

All of the strands in this rubric sample are simple additive, developmental, or combinations of those two rubric strand designs. As mentioned in chapter 6, the most important consideration in rubric design is not the kind of approach taken or number of approaches to strand development used in any given rubric. The most important consideration in rubric design is how well the resulting rubric strands assess what they are intended to assess. This is the ultimate "gold standard" guiding principle pertinent to the design and implementation of assessment rubrics.

EXAMPLE 2: ADDRESSING STATE AND NATIONAL STANDARDS IN A LONGITUDINAL CASE STUDY ANALYSIS

The guiding principle of designing rubrics to best assess what they are intended to assess applies not only to the approach taken to strand development. It applies to the overall design of the rubric as well. In the second example of integrating standards alignment (table 10.2), state and national standards needed to be addressed by students completing a yearlong case study performed in a clinical setting. Five approaches to rubric strand design

Table 10.2. Clinical Case Study Analysis Questions

Research Subjects and Clinical Context

1. Describe changes in the three research subjects from initial to final observation.
2. Describe relevant changes, if any, to clinical context (personnel, setting, etc.).

Content of Intervention or Treatment Designed

3. What were the goals and objectives of the intervention or treatment?
4. How were state standards components integrated into the intervention or treatment?
5. How were national standards integrated into the intervention or treatment?
6. How was technology integrated into the intervention or treatment?

Effectiveness of Intervention or Treatment Design(s)

7. Did the intervention or treatment fully achieve your desired result?
8. Was the intervention or treatment design effective? Why or why not?
9. What concerns or issues arose during the course of this case study?

Analysis of Subjects' Progress from First to Final Observation and Next Steps

10 What, if anything, would you do differently if you could redo the intervention or treatment?
11. What subsequent goals and next steps were planned for the subjects by the end of the study?
12. Describe individual progress of the three subjects from first to final observation and analysis.

Compare/Contrast Clinical Skills, First to Final Observation

13. Compare/contrast your clinical skills from the first to the final observation and analysis.

Compare/Contrast Content Knowledge, First to Final Observation

14. Compare/contrast your content knowledge from the first to the final observation and analysis.

were used: alignment based (strand B), quality enhanced (strands D and F), quality enhanced combined with simple additive (strands C and E), quantity structured (strand G), and de facto simple additive (strand A).

The rubric strands were developed to assist clinical faculty in assessing responses to questions pertaining to a yearlong case study analysis project, grouped by general topic or individual, as displayed in table 10.2. The strands in the rubric were developed within a context of standards-based require-ments for candidates to self-assess and reflect on specific components of their professional growth.

Because of the way the questions are grouped and function in the rubric strands, a case could be made for some of the strands being more holistic than analytic. This would especially be the case if hard-and-fast distinctions between the two are applied. Again, the important consideration here is not whether an individual strand is purely analytic or purely holistic. The important consideration is how well the standards-focused rubric strands assess what they are intended to assess.

Instructions that were provided to students preparing to write the final reflective analysis for the yearlong case study are included here:

> Final product will consist of narrative responses to the questions below, as described in the handbook. If one of your three research subjects moved during the year, respond to these questions for the remaining two subjects and answer the questions as they pertain to the third research subject as best you can. Case study analysis formatting: Single space, with a double space between questions in boldface and paragraphs, using Times New Roman 12-point font and 1" margins. Remember to include APA cover page and separate references page.

The standards-based questions designed to guide the analysis of the case study are included in table 10.2; the assessment rubric used to assess responses to the questions may be found in table 10.3. Note that this assessment rubric is organized so that the most-desired outcome is closest to the standards-focused descriptor for the rubric strand and the far left criterion column carries the highest potential number of points. As previously stated, rubric strands can be organized from high value to low or from low to high. Either is correct, as long as assessors and assessees are clear on the organizational format used so there is no confusion when assigning or reading rubric scores.

The resulting standards-focused rubric was used to assess the standards-based reflective analysis questions students used to summarize their yearlong work in a case study project. Using the observable elements under the pertinent standards as the basis for rubric strand descriptors provided a means not only to operationalize the standards in applied practice but to assess the resulting implementation.

KEY CONSIDERATIONS: DEVELOPING
STANDARDS-ALIGNED RUBRICS AND RUBRIC STRANDS

- Use the standards to develop the descriptors that determine the strands.
- Overriding standards are often broken out into bulleted lists of specific elements, attributes, skills, or expected professional competencies.
- Observable attributes can easily be turned into descriptors for use in a performance-focused or product-focused rubric.
- Add to the standards, providing college- or university-specific competencies.

Table 10.3. Yearlong Case Study Analysis (21 Possible Points)

Component	3	2	1	0
A. Research Subjects (Demographics, Strengths/Areas of Concern) and Clinical Context (Questions 1, 2)	Specific data-focused descriptions of subjects, clinical setting, and changes between initial and final observations.	Clear descriptions of subjects, clinical setting, and changes between initial and final observations.	Minimal or nonspecific descriptions of subjects, clinical setting, or changes between initial and final observations.	Minimal or nonspecific descriptions of subjects, clinical setting, and changes between initial and final observations.
B. Content of Intervention or Treatment Designed (Questions 3, 4, 5, 6)	Clear goals and objectives, with examples of systemic integration of state and national standards.	Clear goals and objectives, with integration of state and national standards.	Goals and objectives unclear or not aligned with state or national standards.	Goals and objectives unclear and not aligned with state and national standards.
C. Effectiveness of Intervention or Treatment Designed (Questions 7, 8, 9)	Strong analysis of specific factors contributing to effectiveness, progress of subjects, concerns or issues if applicable, and how they were addressed.	Strong analysis of overall effectiveness, progress of subjects, concerns or issues if applicable, and how they were addressed.	Vague analysis of effectiveness, progress of subjects, or presence of concerns or issues not addressed.	Effectiveness not analyzed and/or unclear impact on subjects; presence of concerns or issues not addressed.
D. Analysis of Subjects' Progress from First to Final Observation and Next Steps (Questions 10, 11, 12)	Specific analysis of subjects' progress since first observation with specific suggestions for continued progress.	Analysis of subjects' progress since first observation with suggestions for continued progress.	Vague analysis of subjects' progress since first observation with nonspecific suggestions for continued progress.	No analysis of subjects' progress since first observation or no suggestions for continued progress.
E. Compare/Contrast Clinical Skills, First to Final Observation (Question 13)	Efficacy in specific clinical skills and professional development addressed with specific examples and overall summary.	Efficacy in clinical skills and professional development addressed with overall summary.	Nonspecific analysis of efficacy in clinical skills or professional development, or vague overall summary.	No mention of clinical skills or professional development, or no overall summary.
F. Compare/Contrast Content Knowledge, First to Final Observation (Question 14)	Specific analysis of growth in content knowledge with case-based examples.	Specific analysis of growth in content knowledge.	Nonspecific analysis of growth in content knowledge or no emphasis on self-selected content area.	No analysis of growth in content knowledge.
G. Edited Copy	0–2 typo, APA format, or mechanical errors	3–5 typo, APA format, or mechanical errors	6–8 typo, APA format, or mechanical errors	>8 typo, APA, format, or mechanical errors

- Maintain interactive working relationships with graduates and professionals in local and online communities to provide world-of-practice reality checks on programming components.
- Field-based practitioners are often uniquely positioned to assist in determining the professional competencies that need to be demonstrated.

11

Additional Rubric Uses

Assessment rubrics have been used primarily to assist evaluators in making objective decisions regarding the quality and subsequent scoring of student work. That element of objective decision making brings potential for additional applications requiring the same degree of objectivity in assessment tasks other than those pertaining to student work.

One of the most important and potentially long-lasting decisions a college or university faculty can make is that of seeking and hiring faculty members, whether full-time contracted, tenure track, term, or part-time/adjunct. As anyone who has been intimately involved with these processes knows, they can be politically charged to say the least. The process can pit search committee, faculty members, and administrators against each other under the deceptively innocent motive of "finding a good fit for the position." Any process related to seeking, hiring, and retaining personnel is only as good and as ethical as the extent to which the agreed-upon steps of that process are followed or enforced.

Errors can occur inadvertently, as was the case for a former colleague when seeking an initial tenure-track position. She learned many years later, while adding a copy of an updated certification to her personnel file, that she did not make an initial paper cut for the position she was eventually offered. A search committee member, probably tired from wading through multiple application packets, recorded that she had no college teaching experience and had her doctorate for three years when in fact her doctorate had been recent and she had three years of college teaching experience.

That error was corrected on a second look at the applications but may have cost her an initial full-time academic job if it had not been caught. Errors can also result from manipulations of the process, or they can simply stem from

143

seeing too many application materials in too short a time and having applicant characteristics or qualifications blur as a result.

Rubrics can be used to make the evaluation of application materials more objective and help ensure that candidates' qualifications are accurately noted and categorized. In this chapter, this will be demonstrated with an actual position advertisement. It was borrowed from the public-access job site www. higheredjobs.org, using the pseudonym of "State U" with any other identifying characteristics omitted or also replaced with pseudonyms.

APPLYING THE RUBRIC DESIGN STEPS

The initial step (*Step 1*) in rubric design is to clearly identify the goal of the assessment task. Although in this case a rubric will be designed to aid in an interview process, it is actually a product—a hard copy or electronic set of application materials—that will be assessed. The goal is to help ensure an objective, criterion-based initial evaluation, or "paper cut," of job candidates' application materials.

Is a rubric an effective and efficient option for this assessment purpose (*Step 2*)? There is a clearly defined set of products, in this case a cover letter, a vita, transcripts, a writing sample, and three letters of recommendation. The assessment task does not involve simple dichotomous components. Yes, if one of the five components is not submitted it is a de facto yes-or-no issue, but that can be accounted for in the rubric design.

Are the variables expressed in terms of limited responses or one correct answer? No. Therein lies the challenge. It would be a much easier assessment task if this were the case. Candidates will be placed in a ranked list but that will be done based on the rubric scores. The five components will all be provided in response to what are essentially open-ended questions. There will be correct answers embedded and some answers will be "more correct" than others, which is what the rubric is intended to help us explore.

Is a rubric a viable option for this assessment task? Yes. The components to be assessed (*Step 3*) are clearly identified and need to be considered individually. Therefore, an analytic rubric will be designed.

One of the potential reasons for the use of a rubric, as mentioned previously in this book, is to help compare and contrast the relative merits of two or more courses of action. That applies in this case, with the course of action ultimately being the offer of employment to a new faculty member. A rubric can be used to assess potential candidates as represented on paper and may also be used as an assessment tool during a telephone or onsite interview. The recruitment process actually begins with the drafting of a position description in which what is omitted can be as important as what is included. For purposes of this example, the position description for a tenure-track professor of history has already been drafted (see table 11.1).

Step 4 in rubric design calls for determining the components to be assessed. Two areas will need to be addressed in the rubric: the qualifications, which will include information from the introductory position description, and the required application packet materials listed in the application procedure section of the position description. The qualifications include the following (each qualification will be considered individually in order to explore the options inherent in each):

- A Ph.D. in history by August [next year] is required.
- Academic preparation and ability to teach in the areas mentioned in the position description.
- Familiarity with recognized best practices in teaching and an interest in using and developing innovative instructional technologies to promote student learning.
- The successful candidate should be able to effectively interact with a wide and diverse range of students.
- Preference will be given to candidates with competency in a language appropriate to the field.

Step 5 in the selection process involves determining the number of rubric columns, the column descriptors if used, and the numerical rating or other scoring system. A four-column rubric was selected to allow for a target qualification level (2), a level that exceeds the target expectation (3), and a level of less than optimal qualifications (1), as well as levels that do not meet qualifications (0). Column headings will be simply titled with numbers as indicated.

That brings the rubric design process to *step 6*. This step involves the heart of the process: writing the rubric strands by drafting observable assessment cell language for each intersection of descriptor criterion and rating.

DEVELOPMENT OF THE RUBRIC STRANDS

First qualification: a Ph.D. in history is required by August of next year. At first glance, this component would be a dichotomous strand, as in table 11.2. However, if another strength of rubrics is considered, that they help to define specific points on a continuum, it is possible to consider some of the possibilities between those two dichotomous points.

Table 11.1.   Position Description: Tenure-Track Assistant Professor of History

DEPARTMENT OF HISTORY, COLLEGE OF HUMANITIES

Tenure-Track Position in 19th-Century United States History

The History Department at State U invites applications for a tenure-track assistant
professor in 19th-century United States history with an emphasis in public history
and a preferred subfield in U.S. borderlands.

Position:

The new State U faculty member will teach survey courses in United States
history, undergraduate and graduate courses in public history and other areas of
specialization, and courses in historical writing, theory, and methods. The department
has a particular interest in developing its capabilities in historic preservation, digital
history, and new media. Positive tenure and promotion decisions require excellent
teaching, research, peer-reviewed publication, and participation in the broader
disciplinary community.

Qualifications:

– A Ph.D. in history by August [next year] is required.

– Academic preparation and ability to teach in the areas mentioned above.

– Familiarity with recognized best practices in teaching and an interest in using and
developing innovative instructional technologies to promote student learning.

– The successful candidate should be able to effectively interact with a wide and
diverse range of students.

– Preference will be given to candidates with competency in a language appropriate to
the field.

Appointment Date: August [next year]

Application Procedure:

Please submit (1) a cover letter describing teaching and research experiences and
interest, (2) a vita, (3) a copy of graduate transcripts, (4) a writing sample, and (5)
three letters of recommendation—online or via hard copies—to:

Dr. Meg Selke, Chair

Department of History, State U

Application Deadline:

All application materials, including letters of recommendation, must be received
by September 15, [this year]. The search committee will interview prospective
candidates during the fall semester of [this year].

Whether or not those inner possibilities are viable and acceptable must be
determined by the designers of the rubric. One way in which gradations of
this criterion could be expressed appears as an incremental rubric strand in
table 11.3.

In this rubric strand, the preferred and specified means of meeting the requirement appears in rubric column 2. If a dissertation is already defended, it

Table 11.2. Dichotomous Treatment of First Qualification

Descriptor:	0	1	2	3
Required Qualifications Ph.D. in history by August [next year]	Ph.D. in history not anticipated by August [next year]	←	→	Ph.D. in history anticipated by August [next year]

is very likely the candidate will have graduated within a year. Not all defenses are successful, but if the defense has been scheduled, especially a year prior to the following August, it is very likely the candidate will complete the doctoral degree by the following August.

If the dissertation defense has not yet been scheduled, especially as it gets closer to the following August, it becomes increasingly unlikely the candidate will complete a doctoral degree in the time limit specified. However, if the candidate's advisor writes a letter of reference in which the desired timeline is indicated as able to be met, a ranking of 1 is assigned. In keeping with the spirit of that requirement, any potential candidates must have a Ph.D. in History by August of next year.

The only thing better than anticipated completion by the following August would be for a candidate to have already earned a Ph.D. in history. So the cell language in the third column indicates an "exceeds requirements" level for the strand.

Table 11.3. First Qualification: Incremental Approach to Ph.D. Requirement

Descriptor:	0	1	2	3
Required Qualifications Ph.D. in History by August [next year]	Ph.D. in history anticipated by August [next year]; dissertation defense not yet scheduled	Ph.D. in history anticipated by August [next year]; dissertation defense not yet scheduled; advisor provides reference assuring progress	Ph.D. in history anticipated by August [next year]; dissertation defended or defense scheduled	An earned Ph.D. in history at time of application

The second qualification to be addressed is that of academic preparation and ability to teach in the following areas: United States history, public history, other areas of specialization, and courses in historical writing, theory, and methods. The department also has a particular interest in developing its capabilities in historic preservation, digital history, and new media. There are several ways to evaluate a candidate's background in these areas.

Designing another they-have-it-or-they-don't dichotomous rubric strand might be the easiest option except for two things. The first is that the qualification has a dual focus—"academic ability" and "ability to teach." The second is the mention of the department's "particular interest" in an additional three areas, which implies the need for weighted scores in these areas.

Consider the dual focal points of academic ability and ability to teach. These criteria would be more easily assessed in a separately headed rubric section with the areas of academic preparation serving as the descriptors. There are three possibilities for academic preparation as defined for purposes of this rubric: Ph.D. coursework, undergraduate or master's coursework, or no coursework in the area. There are five possibilities for college teaching experience: Ph.D.-level teaching experience in the area or outside of the area, undergraduate or master's teaching in or outside of the area, and no college teaching experience.

The intersection of these two sets of possibilities would result in fifteen possible experiential combinations. The matrix in table 11.4 was drafted to account for every possible combination a candidate could present. Each of those *possible* combinations was rated in terms of acceptability as a candidate for this position on a scale from zero to three.

Table 11.4.   Crosstabs Matrix: Possible Combinations of Teaching Experience and Coursework

	Ph.D. teaching exp. in this area	*Ph.D. teaching exp. in another area*	*M.A./ undergrad teaching exp. in this area*	*M.A./ undergrad teaching exp. in another area*	*No teaching experience yet*
Ph.D. coursework in this area	3	3	3	2	1
M.A./undergrad coursework in this area	–	1	0	0	0
No coursework in this area	–	0	0	0	0

Step 7 in rubric construction calls for the addition of headings, if appropriate. In this case, these ratings above were used to design not section headings but the individual column headings for this section of the rubric accounting for every *probable* combination (see table 11.5). The provision of two options in columns one through three provides flexibility without compromising equitable application of the rubric.

Some of the column headings do differentiate between college teaching—which refers to undergraduate, master's-level, or other predoctoral-level teaching experience—and Ph.D. teaching. (In the finished rubric, it would probably be advisable to add a code key as a footnote explaining those differences.) The rationale is that a candidate with experience teaching doctoral-level courses would be better prepared to teach a wider range of courses, from undergraduate to doctoral.

Table 11.5. Second Qualification: Academic Preparation and Teaching Experience

Descriptor:	0	1	2	3
Academic Preparation and Teaching Experience	No or only M.A./ undergrad coursework in area and no college teaching yet	Undergrad or master's coursework in this area and college teaching in another area Or Ph.D. coursework but no college teaching yet	Undergrad or master's coursework in this area and college teaching in this or another area Or Ph.D. coursework and college teaching in another area	Ph.D. coursework and college teaching experience in this area Or Undergrad/ M.A. coursework in this area and Ph.D. teaching in another area
U.S. History Public History Historical Writing/ Theory/ Methods Other Areas of Specialization Historic Preservation Digital History New Media				

In regard to scoring all of the academic preparation areas used as descriptors, the easiest option would be to work with the numerical scores of 0–3 that were set up for the columns in this rubric. If that is done, however, the aspect of academic preparation and teaching experience may have a disproportionate impact on a candidate's overall score. In addition, using 0–3 for all academic preparation and teaching descriptors does not account for the emphasis the narrative position advertisement places on historic preservation, digital history, and new media.

Step 8 in rubric construction raises the question of whether or not weightings would be helpful in balancing the impact of the various components in the rubric on composite rubric scores. Rather than weighting those three components double, and in an attempt to balance the impact of these descriptor scores on the remainder of the rubric, these three descriptors will be weighted as indicated. The components of U.S. history, public history, other areas of specialization, and historical writing, theory, and methods will be rated half ($\times$ .50) of the column scores.

The third qualification is a bit of a challenge because familiarity is essentially a disposition rather than a behavior that can be verified in written application materials. Answers to questions in a telephone or onsite interview, or questions asked of references in follow-up contacts, would be better means of assessing this component. However, the ways in which prospective can-

Table 11.6.   Third and Fourth Qualifications: Familiarity with Best Practices in Teaching and Innovative Technology

Descriptor:	0	1	2	3
Familiarity with Recognized Best Practices in Teaching	Best practices not addressed or comments indicate lack of familiarity with current best practices	Familiarity demonstrated via mention of commitment to techniques in cover letter	Familiarity demonstrated via specific theorists and techniques mentioned in cover letter	Familiarity demonstrated via application examples and specific theorists and techniques mentioned in cover letter
Interest in Using and Developing Innovative Instructional Technologies to Promote Student Learning	No mention of innovative instructional technology in cover letter	Professed commitment to innovative instructional technology without example(s) in cover letter	Example(s) of general innovative instructional technology in cover letter	Example(s) of content-specific uses of innovative instructional technology in cover letter

Table 11.7. Qualification 5: Effective Interaction with a Wide and Diverse Range of Students

Descriptor:	0	1	2	3
Effectively Interact with a Wide and Diverse Range of Students	No experience yet with student interaction or comments give rise to questions regarding comfort with diversity	No experience yet with student interaction; potential supported by reference(s)	College teaching experience supported by reference(s)	College teaching experience supported by reference(s) with strong student and peer reviews

didates approach this component in a cover letter, and how they define "best practices," would also provide valuable information that can be assessed via the rubric strand in table 11.6.

A similar reasoning process was used to assess the fourth qualification: candidates' interest in the use and development of innovative instructional technologies to facilitate student learning. The rubric strand for this qualification (see table 11.6) was set up to look for evidence of this component as it was discussed in each applicant's cover letter.

The fifth qualification contains several terms that are somewhat subjective in nature, including "effectively" and "wide and diverse range." Instead of looking for evidence solely in the cover letter, insight regarding this qualification will be sought in candidates' letters of reference, as indicated in the strand in table 11.7.

There are a couple ways in which the sixth qualification could be handled. The strand itself is set up to recognize bilingual ability and also any candidates who exceed that by being multilingual (see table 11.8). Limited bilingual ability, or lack of same, is clearly specified. Once the strand has been constructed, one option would be to treat this strand simply as another in the rubric and add the score on this strand to the scores accumulated so far.

Table 11.8. Sixth Qualification: Bilingual Competence in a Field-Appropriate Language

Preferred Qualifications	0	1	2	3
Competency in a Language Appropriate to the Field	Monolingual	Limited bilingual (e.g., read only) ability	Yes, bilingual	Yes, multilingual

Table 11.9. Candidate Qualification Rubric (33 Possible Points)

Descriptor:	0	1	2	3
Required Qualifications Ph.D. in History by August [next year]	Ph.D. in history anticipated by August [next year]; dissertation defense not yet scheduled	Ph.D. in history anticipated by August [next year]; dissertation defense not yet scheduled; advisor provides reference assuring progress	Ph.D. in history anticipated by August [next year]; dissertation defended or defense scheduled	An earned Ph.D. in history at time of application
Academic Preparation and Teaching Experience Specializations in History:	No or only M.A./ undergrad coursework in area and no college teaching yet	Undergrad or master's coursework in this area and college teaching in another area Or Ph.D. coursework but no college teaching yet	Undergrad or master's coursework in this area and college teaching in this or another area Or Ph.D. coursework and college teaching in another area	Ph.D. coursework and college teaching experience in this area Or Undergrad/M.A. coursework in this area and Ph.D. teaching in another area
U.S. History (× .50) Public History (× .50) Historical Writing/ Theory/Methods (× .50) Historic Preservation (× .50) Digital History (× .50) New Media (× .50)				

Familiarity with Recognized Best Practices in Teaching	Best practices not addressed or comments indicate lack of familiarity with current best practices	Familiarity demonstrated via mention of commitment to techniques in cover letter	Familiarity demonstrated via specific theorists and techniques mentioned in cover letter	Familiarity demonstrated via application examples and specific theorists and techniques mentioned in cover letter
Interest in Using and Developing Innovative Instructional Technologies to Promote Student Learning	No mention of innovative instructional technology in cover letter	Professed commitment to innovative instructional technology without example(s) in cover letter	Example(s) of general innovative instructional technology in cover letter	Example(s) of content-specific uses of innovative instructional technology in cover letter
Effectively Interact with a Wide and Diverse Range of Students	No experience yet with student interaction or comments give rise to questions regarding comfort with diversity	No experience yet with student interaction; potential supported by reference(s)	College teaching experience supported by reference(s)	College teaching experience supported by reference(s) with strong student and peer reviews
Preferred Qualifications				
Competency in a Language Appropriate to the Field	Monolingual	Limited bilingual (e.g., read only) ability	Yes, bilingual	Yes, multilingual
Peer-Reviewed Publications	Dissertation only	1 or more journal articles submitted for publication	1 or more coauthored journal articles published	1 or more sole authored journal articles published
Participation in the Disciplinary Community	Limited participation (e.g., attends conferences)	Membership in student professional organization	Membership in professional organization	Leadership role in professional organization

Another option would be to hold this strand in reserve until the top ten to fifteen candidates have been determined. Once that point is reached, especially if all the composite scores are very close and it is proving difficult to narrow the field of top candidates for telephone or onsite interviews, this rubric strand could be applied only to those candidates to assist in determining final rankings.

The remaining two preferred qualifications could be addressed in much the same way. The elements of peer-reviewed publications and participation in the disciplinary community—as defined by participation in professional organizations—have also been added to the rubric as the last two strands. This results in a rubric with thirty-three possible points.

The final draft of the full rubric may be found in table 11.9. (The option of including the bilingual strand on the full rubric was selected.) Final *draft?* Yes. Because the *ninth* and final *step* is to pilot the rubric—try it out on sample performances or products. Revise the rubric as needed until it works with any kinds of assessment tasks for which it has been designed. Piloting the rubric is essential for several reasons: It needs to be easy to score. All of the terminology in the rubric needs to be unambiguous. Resulting composite scores need to accurately reflect the relative capabilities of candidates in a pool.

Once a rubric is drafted, a corresponding spreadsheet, designed in a format similar to a grade book, can be developed, as demonstrated in table 11.10. Once single copies of the rubric are used to score the application materials of individual candidates, the resulting scores may be entered into the spreadsheet. For example, if the first two candidates' cover letters presented the following information, their rubric scores would be entered as indicated in table 11.10.

Candidate 1 has a Ph.D. in American History with an emphasis in World War II, European and Pacific fronts. The candidate was a T.A. as a doctoral student at a Midwest university, teaching master's level courses in American History to 1875, assisting students in the thesis phase with historical writing, and receiving high student course evaluation scores and supervisor recommendations. The candidate works to apply teaching methods specific to social sciences, is tech savvy, and brings applied experience in digital history and innovative media. The candidate is active in professional organizations and has also submitted a dissertation-based article to a peer-reviewed professional journal and speaks a fairly fluent German, having spent a semester in Austria as an undergraduate.

Candidate 2 has defended a dissertation and will be graduating this spring with a Ph.D. in nineteenth-century world history, an emphasis in public history, and several courses in U.S. borderlands. The candidate has been a full-

Table 11.10. Rubric Score Spreadsheet

Descriptor:	Candidate 1	Candidate 2	Candidate 3	Candidate 4	Candidate 5
Ph.D. in History by August	3	2			
Teaching Experience	2	2			
U.S. History	3	2			
Public History	–	3			
Writing/Theory/ Methods	3	–			
Historic Preservation	–	3			
Digital History	3	–			
New Media	3	3			
Best Practices in Teaching	2	2			
Innovative Technology	3	2			
Interacting with Students	3	2			
Foreign Language	2	1			
Peer-Reviewed Publications	1	3			
Disciplinary Community	2	1			
Total Points:	30 so far	26 so far			

Key: "-": Check transcripts or letters of recommendation for evidence not addressed in the cover letter.

time instructor at a community college, teaching a range of courses in U.S. and world history, and during college held summer jobs involving historic preservation. The candidate attends professional conferences and has published two articles on getting undergraduates interested in history by using virtual field trips and related media-based history-focused technology. The candidate can speak and read a little Spanish and has worked in a school with many first-generation college students from Hispanic backgrounds.

Based on cover letter information alone, the qualifications of the two candidates appeared to be quite similar. However, when the cover letter information was held up to the preestablished requirements as specified in the rubric, one of the candidates—at this point in the process—was found to be a better potential match for the position. In this instance, an example of assessment taking place outside of a classroom setting, a rubric has served the purpose of making what can be an inherently subjective process more objective and criteria focused.

In essence, that brings the focus back full circle to the reasons for rubric use presented in the initial section of this book. The multiple advantages of rubrics permit instructors to monitor progress and recognize mastery. Rubrics also help instructors communicate to students what they have done right, what they have done wrong, and what they specifically need to demonstrate in order to improve their performances or the quality of the work they produce.

It is this author's sincere hope that this book will be useful for university, professional school, college, community college, and upper-level secondary school faculty members wishing to gain a practical, comprehensive working knowledge of rubric design, analysis, and implementation. Refer to each chapter's key considerations for quick reviews. Don't be afraid to experiment and have fun as you develop assessment rubrics (revisit the ice cream sundae process?). Above all, it is hoped that readers enjoy the process of constructing and implementing rubrics. It may take some time, especially at first, and it may be challenging. But isn't that true of most endeavors that are ultimately worthwhile?

Annotated Bibliography

The following list of reviewed resources may be helpful to readers in search of additional rubric examples and related materials pertaining to assessment.

Association for the Assessment of Learning in Higher Education (2012). Retrieved from http://course1.winona.edu/shatfield/air/rubrics.htm.

A select collection of rubrics from institutions around the United States, the AALHE website rubrics address topics such as civil and environmental engineering, ethics, social integration, action research, and art history. The large collection of rubrics also contains suggested strands for use in assessing online discussions, class participation, and teamwork.

Blackboard, Inc. (2011). On demand learning center: Assessing learners. Retrieved from http://ondemand.blackboard.com/assess.htm.

Open-access online videos from Blackboard on a variety of assessment topics. The collection includes a three-minute video on creating and scoring a rubric in the Blackboard system.

California State University (n.d.). Links to examples of scoring rubrics. Retrieved from http://www.calstate.edu/itl/resources/assessment/scoring-rubrics-examples.shtml.

The Institute for Teaching and Learning at CSU provides a webpage that contains links to over forty sites with examples of college-level rubrics (and some PK–12 rubrics) from many disciplines, including but not limited to mathematics, writing, speaking, culture, ethics, engineering, social studies, and problem solving. Site links connect with college-level rubrics on campus websites from California to Alaska to the East Coast.

Clement, M. C. (2011). Three steps to better course evaluations. *The Teaching Professor, 25*(4), 1, 3.

Three areas are addressed: (1) understanding and accepting today's college students, (2) establishing clear criteria for grading, and (3) the importance of early formative feedback. The use and implementation of rubric assessment is addressed within the broader perspective of assessing students productively in order to achieve better course evaluations.

Franker, K. (2012). On-line professional development: Rubrics for teachers. Retrieved from http://www.uwstout.edu/soe/profdev/rubrics.shtml.

This University of Wisconsin–Stout website contains a comprehensive assortment of assessment rubrics, including rubrics for evaluating electronic applications, wikis, podcasts, and multimedia presentations. The rubrics provide sound examples of rubric design but focus on K–12 skill performances and products.

Fresno State University Office of Institutional Effectiveness (2012). Rubric library. Retrieved from http://www.fresnostate.edu/academics/oie/assessment/rubric.html.

Contains PDFs for rubrics in many areas, such as more general instruments to be used to assess oral presentations and critical thinking, as well as assessment tools for specific disciplines, such as a theater arts writing rubric. A useful set of recommendations for using rubrics is also provided.

Kappa Omicron Nu (2009). Rubric samples for higher education. Retrieved from: http://rubrics.kon.org/.

The site features college-focused rubrics for assessing undergraduate research, student organizations, and student reflections. The advisor-as-teacher model is emphasized, and a rubric for assessing this is provided.

Little, D. (2006, fall). Grading with rubrics: Developing a fair and efficient assessment tool. *Teaching Concerns*. Retrieved from http://trc.virginia.edu/Publications/Teaching_Concerns/Fall_2006/TC_Fall_2006_Little.htm.

Teaching Concerns, a newsletter for faculty and teaching assistants, is provided by the University of Virginia's Teaching Resource Center and is publicly accessible on the Internet. This edition contains a sample rubric, questions for authors to ask when developing rubrics, and five related references, most available online.

Moskal, B. (2000). Scoring rubrics: What, when and how? *Practical Assessment, Research & Evaluation, 7*(3). Retrieved from http://pareonline.net/getvn.asp?v=7&n=3.

The author of this article is affiliated with the Colorado School of Mines and provides an introduction to rubrics for scoring student work. Descriptions of different types of scoring rubrics and ways of developing rubrics are included.

Professional and Organizational Development Network in Higher Education (n.d.). Rubrics: WikiPODia. Retrieved from https://sites.google.com/a/pod-network.org/wikipodia/Home/topics-for-discussion/Rubrics.

An introduction to rubrics at the college and university level is provided, with multiple guides to creating, using, and assessing with rubrics. Includes links to many other rubric examples and resources; some are content-area specific.

RubiStar (2012). Create rubrics for your project-based learning activities. Retrieved from http://rubistar.4teachers.org/index.php.

This site contains an online tutorial and templates for creating rubrics for a wide variety of learning activities. Users must log in, but use of the site is free of charge, users can store partially or fully designed rubrics, and interactive rubrics can be created.

Squidoo (2012). Reduce hassles, teach smarter—rubrics for college. Retrieved from http://www.squidoo.com/TeachCollege2.

This website features rubrics with three or four levels. Several college-focused rubrics are provided, including an example of a rubric on preparation for going to court, applicable to a unit in business law.

Stevens, D., & Levi, A. (2008). Introduction to rubrics: An assessment tool to save grading time, convey effective feedback and promote student learning. Retrieved from http://www.styluspub.com/resources/introductiontorubrics.aspx.

A companion website to their book of the same name, this site provides three-level and four-level rubric templates. An example of a class discussion rubric is included in addition to a discussion board on which participants can share rubrics and request feedback from other rubric developers.

Texas Christian University (2012). Rubrics. Retrieved from http://www.cte. tcu.edu/learningoutcomes_grading.htm.

The Koehler Center for Teaching Excellence at TCU has assembled an online collection of college and university assessment rubrics from United States and Canadian institutions. Assessment topics include but are not limited to science papers, primary trait analysis, and critical thinking. There are also links to rubric tutorials and rubric generators.

Index

About the Author

Mary J. Goggins Selke, Ph.D., is a career-long teacher and teacher educator. She earned her baccalaureate degree in vocal music with teaching certification from the University of Wisconsin–Milwaukee, her M.Ed. in professional development from Cardinal Stritch University, and her Ph.D. in Educational Administration and Supervision from Marquette University. Leadership positions include serving as an elementary principal, managing a university student-teaching center, serving as chair of an education department, and working with online curriculum design. She is an active member of the Association of Teacher Educators, where she initiated the graduate research forum and is the founding chair of the ATE SIG for Educational Leadership. Her research interests include professional induction, teacher leadership, career phases of school administrators, and the applications of performance-based assessment.

Outside of the professional realm, Dr. Goggins Selke cherishes musical performance and music ministry and enjoys travel, theater, reading, baking, swimming, gardening, adding to her sea shell collection, spending time with family and friends—and indulging the pursuit of chocolate that rates top rubric scores.